Unlimited Riches

Unlimited Riches

Making Your Fortune in Real Estate Investing

ROBERT SHEMIN

John Wiley & Sons, Inc.

Published by John Wiley & Sons, Inc., Hoboken, New Jersey
Published simultaneously in Canada

For general information on our other products and services, or technical support, please contact our Customer Care Department within the United States at 800-762-2974, outside the United States at 317-572-3993 or fax 317-572-4002.

Wiley also publishes its books in a variety of electronic formats. Some content that appears in print may not be available in electronic books.

Library of Congress Cataloging-in-Publication Data:

Shemin, Robert, 1963–
    Unlimited riches : making your fortune in real estate investing / Robert Shemin
       p. cm.
    Includes index.
    ISBN 0-471-25062-7 (cloth : alk. paper)
    1. Real estate investment. 2. Investments. I. Title

    HD255 .S486 2002
    332.63'24–dc21

                                                                    2002068990

Printed in the United States of America

10 9 8 7 6 5 4 3 2 1

To Alexander: Everything that I do, I do thinking about you.

CONTENTS

Contents

Thanks so much, Michael Hamilton, John Wiley & Sons, Inc., for allowing me this great opportunity to write *Unlimited Riches: Making Your Fortune in Real Estate Investing.*

There is no way that this project would be possible without Barbara McNichol, who assisted in writing this book, and proof-reader Faye Q. Heimerl.

I would also like to thank my parents Jules and Lillian Shemin for their help and support. Thank you, Dad, for being the smartest and most inspirational businessperson I have ever known.

Once again, here is to you Janie Hataway. Thank you Paul Bauer, without whom my real estate speaking career would not be what it is today.

I also must express my appreciation for Jack Bufkin, who starts each of my business days with a lot of laughs.

And to the readers: Happy investing.

Indecision is the thief of opportunity.
—JIM ROHN

Getting Started

When I started in real estate, I thought there was only one way to do real estate: Borrow money, buy property, put my name on the title, rent it, put up with tenants, have the tenants pay off the costs, and make money over time. With luck, I would make money every month.

Then I learned how to flip property, fix it up and sell it, or lease-option it. I also learned that I did not have to use my own money or credit to buy homes. Most people, including myself sometimes, have no hands-on experience in the subject matter about which they are giving advice. You should seek advice only from experts. Even my mother would say, "Robert, this no-money-down stuff, I don't buy it; I don't believe it can be true." Now, every time I go to my mother's house for dinner, she says, "Robert, I've seen you on

TV and [in] newspapers and books. Why do you keep telling people you can buy property without using your own money or credit? Stop it!" She still will not believe me. She's an excellent expert at being a mom. However, she hasn't done any real estate investing. Yet, for the last 200 properties that I have bought, sold, and made money with, I have not used one penny of my own money or one point of my own credit. That is true. You are going to learn ways to do that, too.

The concepts I present here work for everything: houses, duplexes, land, commercial buildings, apartment buildings, trailer parks, whatever you are interested in. Small properties, big ones, cheap ones, and expensive ones. There is a big difference between a $1 million property and a $100,000 property, but the process and paperwork for buying and selling them is exactly the same.

As a full-time real estate investor, I have bought or sold about 500 properties in the last five or six years. At one time, I had more than 300 tenants whom I managed for years, and I still manage some. I constantly buy, flip, lease-option, and manage properties.

I decided that working at a job for 50 years and waiting for retirement in a nice place was not for me. I therefore recently purchased some nice places in South Beach, Florida, where a lot of people vacation. People are flipping expensive properties there. I also have some real estate deals in Costa Rica and in Latin America, where I like to travel. Once you learn how to do this, you can go anywhere. My students have demonstrated that the concepts in this book work in the two most expensive real estate markets in the world: San Francisco and Manhattan. They also work in your town. If they do not work exactly where you are, just go 35 minutes up the road.

Overnight Successes

I am from Nashville, Tennessee. My papa plays the banjo, and my mama plays the fiddle (just kidding). Nashville is where talented people go and sometimes become overnight successes. Garth Brooks, my neighbor for 5 years, became an overnight success after getting kicked out of every record company and having to play on street corners for 12 years. That kind of overnight success applies to me, too.

About 10 years ago, I did not know a thing about real estate and did not want to. I was a financial consultant working for a New York financial planning firm. Our clients had to have $3 million or $5 million to invest with us, which meant they had $9 million or $10 million total.

What Changed My Mind

One day while working for a financial planning firm, I was sent to visit an older couple living in Nashville. They had a beat-up old office and drove a dumpy pickup truck. They looked like poor, uneducated bums. It appeared that they could not even read or write well. I talked with them and learned that they did not have computers, they did not understand advanced finance, and they did not even understand a term like *return on investments.* "Obviously, you are not qualified to work with my firm," I said as I started to leave the old gentleman's office. He replied, "Come over here, Sonny." He picked up a book and paused, "When I was working about 25 years ago and making no money, I started buying little houses without using any of my own money. I'd fix them up, rent them, and sell them." Then he opened his big old accounting book, the kind with old ledger sheets and the lines going across the page. He kept all of his own records using just that book and a pencil. (He still does.) He owned 125 houses, all paid for, and showed me he had $65,000 a month coming in. He and his wife would go on vacation for six months every year. He looked me in the eye, "Robert, how's your job?"

All of a sudden, young cocky Robert got very interested in this man's profession: real estate. In the back of my mind, I thought,

"If this 80-year-old guy can do it, I can too." He still picks up rent checks every day and still goes out and makes more deals. He certainly does not have to. For him, real estate is fun.

This really got my attention, so I followed him around for several months. I also interviewed 200 other investors and 200 tenants. I put together a big plan for my real estate business, and guess what I did with it for several months afterward? Nothing! As the expression goes, "I was a thinkin' about it. I was a fixin' to do something." That went on for about eight months. During that time, I looked at about 150 properties. Of those, at least 50 were great deals, but I did not understand flipping and lease optioning, so I did not take action. I passed by several hundred thousand dollars in profits.

What kept me from going after those profits? Fear. (More precisely, I was scared to death!) However, I did finally make an offer on a duplex, and it was accepted. That scared me, too. How would I close on it? . . . I borrowed the money and bought that duplex. At that time, my written plan was to buy 12 duplexes and retire. I figured each one would draw from $300 to $500 a month in cash flow, which I could live on. That old couple's success got me started.

My First Investment Duplex

Because I have a form of dyslexia, I cannot do a lot of things that people take for granted. For example, I cannot follow directions to put together a four-year-old child's toy. I cannot read maps. Certain mathematical things I cannot do. Even though I have rehabbed at least 500 houses, I know *absolutely nothing* about construction or repairs. When contractors talk about roof trusses, drywall, and wires, it is like they are speaking Chinese or Greek. That language simply makes no sense in my brain.

When I bought my first duplex, I could not find it because I cannot use maps. People still do not understand that. For a day and a half, I drove around Hermitage, Tennessee, looking for my duplex. They all looked the same. I called the broker and said, "I can't find the property I just closed on. Where is it?" I was so embarrassed. He actually met me and drove me to it.

Fortunately, however, I did find my first duplex, rented it out, and that worked. Then I bought my 12 duplexes. After a year and a half, I quit my job and retired; for one year, I did not do anything because I had about $4,000 or $5,000 of tax-free money coming in every month. Then I thought, "Gee, if it works with 12 duplexes, it's got to work with 24 or 25, and if it works with 25, it should work with 50, and if works with 50, it has got to work with 100, 200, and 300 properties." (I do have help, one person who helps me manage all of my properties, along with a part-time secretary.)

Instead of learning 1 way to make money in real estate, you will learn about 10 ways. You may not use them all, but pick up a few of them and get started.

Why Real Estate Investing?

Maybe you want to buy your own home and learn how to save thousands of dollars on the transaction. Maybe you realize there is no job security in the United States (layoffs, reengineering, and early retirement all equal being fired), so you want to create your own business. Even if you have a great job and things are going well, if you are wealthy and successful, I still challenge you to do real estate investing on the side.

You live somewhere right now. If you pay rent, you are probably making someone wealthy. You are contributing to someone else's investments and security, not yours. You pay your rent on time and thank your landlord, but at the end of the year, you have nothing to show for it except 12 canceled checks.

If you own a home, you are already a real estate investor. You probably know somebody—a friend, a relative, a coworker, a grandparent, an uncle, or an aunt—who has made a lot of money in real estate, often by accident. Most people spend 40 to 50 hours a week stressed out, working to make $40,000 a year and then, with one real estate deal, they make $40,000 almost by accident in a short amount of time.

If these results appeal to you, you can do it, too! You simply need three things:

1. Desire
2. Basic knowledge and information
3. Persistent action

This book can give you all of the basic information that you need to get started. Make this book the catalyst to get you started and to find within yourself the desire to succeed. I hope this book encourages you to start taking persistent actions toward becoming a real estate investor with various sources of income.

Happy investing!

Act as if it were impossible to fail.
—DOROTHEA BRANDE

Real Estate: The Best Wealth Builder in the Universe

Why is real estate investing the best wealth builder in the universe? The answer is simple: Everyone needs a place to live, and real estate values usually go up over time. I can assure you that, in the next 20 years, your real estate property will probably double, triple, perhaps even quadruple in value. If you are in a hot market, it might even go up 10 to 20 times.

When is the time to get into real estate investing? Yesterday. Real estate increases its value to build wealth, but there are other reasons why real estate investing, compared with any other investing, is the best.

Income, Wealth, and Advantages

Here are five advantages of investing in real estate, the best wealth builder in the universe, as it leads to wealth for you.

1. *Real estate increases your net worth.* One of real estate's biggest advantages is how it can increase your net worth instantly because you can buy property *below* market value. For example, if you find a property that is worth $500,000 and a motivated seller who is willing to let it go for $300,000, you put it under contract for $300,000 (about 60 percent of its worth), then borrow all $300,000, close the deal, and become the owner of this property. You borrowed all of the money to make this happen; you did not use your own. The minute you own this property, your bank and your financial statement say you have an asset worth $500,000 and a $300,000 loan against it. Congratulations. Your net worth just went up $200,000.

   Here is a more conservative example. In my first real estate deal, I bought a duplex that was worth $60,000 for $40,000— not a home-run deal, certainly not a grand slam—but as soon as I bought the duplex, my net worth went up $20,000. Property value ($60,000) minus property cost ($40,000) equals gain in net worth ($20,000).

   This concept is hard for most Americans to understand because usually when they buy something big (e.g., a new car, television, jewelry, stereo), their net worth goes down instantly. The $30,000 car I bought goes down in value to $20,000; therefore, my net worth decreases by $10,000. However, if you buy real estate correctly, your net worth goes up because it appreciates over time, unlike most items that depreciate.

2. *Real estate generates income from holding properties.* Rental property (a house, commercial property, or an apartment building) is unique because your tenants pay off your debt on that real estate. If you own rental property with $500 monthly mortgage payments and $800 monthly rental income, you

end up with a cash flow of $300, which is extra money in your pocket. The cash will likely be tax-free because of depreciation and write-offs. Your tenants actually pay off your mortgage debt and, in 10 to 30 years (depending on the length of your loan), that debt will disappear and your net worth will go up again.

Residual income creates happiness (RICH) is the concept in which you, your family, and your estate (after you die) will benefit from residual income because the rent keeps coming in.

3. *With real estate, you can pay less than what the property is worth.* By looking for deals, you can buy real estate that is priced at 20 to 50 percent of what it it is worth. This means you seek $100,000 properties that you can buy for, say, $70,000. Compare that with the stock market. Can you find stock that is worth $100 and pay $70 for it? No. You pay $70, the market value, then pray it goes up to $100. It could hold at $70 for a year, then go up, or it could go down because that's the nature of the stock market. You cannot buy stocks below market value like you can real estate.

4. *Real estate offers tax advantages.* The third big advantage of real estate investing is how it affects your tax obligations. If you have a traditional job with a traditional paycheck, you are entitled to very few tax write-offs or deductions. However, in real estate or any business you own, you can write off a wide array of expenses, including phone calls and a portion of your business meals. Owning real estate provides the opportunity to write off most of your mortgage interest and property depreciation.

5. *You do not need cash or credit to get into real estate.* In the stock market, you require most or all of your cash up front to purchase stocks. If you want to buy a $100 stock, you have to pay $100 cash. Some banks or brokerage houses will lend you half of the money to buy stock, but you will still have to come up with the other half.

In real estate investing, if you find a property selling for

$70,000 that is worth $100,000, you can borrow the entire $70,000. If you have good credit, almost any bank or mortgage company will lend you 70 percent ($70,000) to buy the $100,000 property. If you do not have cash or good credit, you can find hard moneylenders who will lend money—in return for charging a high interest rate. They will lend you $70,000 for a property worth $100,000 without caring if you pay them back, because if you do not pay them, they take your property.

In any business or investment, especially real estate, you can use either your own money (YOM) or other people's money (OPM). *Owner's terms* is an example of OPM. If you buy a house and the owner lends you money to purchase instead of your having to go a bank, you are using the owner's money.

What if you do not have enough money or credit to invest, but have enough knowledge to be a successful real estate investor? Then look for investors (i.e., people with money or good credit) who can borrow at great rates. These investors may have a lot of cash or retirement accounts that they are tired of putting into stocks and are seeking other ways to invest. You might convince them to invest with you if you have a good business plan and have already had some business success. Investors put in the money while you put in the knowledge and time.

An Overview of the Road to Unlimited Riches in Real Estate

During my first several years of real estate investing, I knew of only one way to make money in real estate—buying and holding; that is, buying and renting property, and collecting rents. Then I learned about flipping, lease optioning, referring contractors and legal services, and so on. I started getting little checks, then medium-sized checks, and finally big checks.

You can do the same. All you have to decide is how many checks you want from how many sources. Open your mind to not only

Examples of OPM Financing

Mr. R. in Florida says his entire family works in real estate. He himself owns hundreds of beautiful properties. However, Mr. R.'s name is not on any deeds, and he does not have any liability, because he has partners and investors (e.g., doctors, lawyers, accountants, bankers) whose names are on the deeds. He discloses every agreement in writing. He does not owe a cent to anyone. When he sells his houses, he earns from $20,000 up to $100,000, and the investors get their money back plus one-half of the profits.

I know a full-time student who makes between $80,000 and $120,000 a year as a part-time real estate investor. He digs up a good deal, puts a property under contract, finds investors, buys the property with their money, fixes it up, then sells it for a profit anywhere in the range of $5,000 to $12,000.

one, two, or three avenues of income, but to multiple avenues of real estate income. Start with one way and, as your career progresses, you will want to add more.

Being a Real Estate Agent

What source of income first comes to mind when *real estate* is mentioned? Making money as a real estate agent or broker, the people who put buyers and sellers together and carry offers between them. The average real estate commission in the United States is generally between 5 and 8 percent of the sale. For example, if a sales price is $100,000 with a 6 percent commission, the agent or broker earns $6,000. Often, however, there are two agent/brokers, one representing the buyer and the other representing the seller, so the commission gets split, dispersing $3,000 to each.

The disadvantages of being a real estate agent/broker include a requirement to be licensed, meet educational standards, pay fees, and carry liability insurance coverage.

Of course, being an agent/broker has an advantage. You have access to the multiple listing service (MLS), which lists all houses for sale in the retail real estate market. You might have access to a real estate office and its up-to-date technology, and also have contact with other agents and resources who can lead you to sales.

Buying and Holding

Most people associate real estate investing with buying and holding property—a great wealth builder. If you buy wisely, your net worth will go up, and you will have monthly cash flow, property appreciation, and some tax advantages.

Certainly, a disadvantage to the buying-and-holding strategy is dealing with a lot of tenants, many of whom cause problems. I always say that if you do not have problems being a landlord, you do not have enough tenants.

Holding property is a management headache. You have to deal with contractors, constant repairs, liability, insurance, taxes, ongoing costs, and overhead. Still, it is one of the best wealth builders in the world. Because of all these variables, I advise against buying and holding property for your first 6 to 12 months of real estate investing, but buy and hold it as time goes by. Most people should start by flipping property so they don't put their capital or credit at risk.

Buying, Fixing, and Selling

A lot of people start in real estate investing by buying, improving, and selling property. Often, beginning investors make the improvements themselves. They work for six months—what I call hang and bang, drywall, paint, and clean—then they sell it. You can make anywhere from $12,000 to $30,000 on a property, especially if you fix up three or four homes a year. It can be a great business, but understand that it takes a lot of time and work.

Quick Turning, Flipping, or Wholesaling

With quick turning, flipping, or wholesaling, an investor finds a good deal, such as a house worth $100,000 that an owner will sell for less than that amount. Suppose an investor puts this $100,000 home under contract for $70,000. If he or she writes the contract properly and puts in a disclosure and contingency clause, he or she will have little or no risk of losing money over this transaction. Shortly after buying the house for $70,000, the investor sells it for $80,000. He or she makes $10,000—a basic wholesale, flip, or quick-turn deal.

The advantage of this income source is that you do not use any of your own money or credit—you get paid for finding deals. The disadvantage is an uncertain future, so you cannot rely on the residual income you would have with the buying-and-holding strategy, and you will have to keep buying and selling property. (See Chapter 7 for more about this strategy.)

Lease Optioning

One of the best ways to control or rent property is through lease optioning. Consider leasing commercial property, houses, vacation property, duplexes, land. Instead of borrowing money to buy a property, thereby getting your name (and all the liability that comes with it) on the deed, consider leasing it for 1 year, 5 years, possibly 50 years.

Think of it this way: If 10 years ago you had locked into 10-year leases on every house in your neighborhood, what leases for $1,000 a month now probably leased for $200 a month a decade ago. Therefore, if you originally leased property for $200 and rented it today for $1,000, you would be making $800 a month.

When you lease with the option to buy, you are locking in the lease for a set number of years as well as having the choice to buy it. Remember, you are not obligated to buy the property, but you do have the right to. When you lease-option property, you control it. You can re-lease it, buy it, option to buy it, or sell it for more than what your option price was. The sky is the limit.

Mortgage Brokering

A long time ago, I was told real estate is not real estate; rather, it is actually finance. This is because with proper financing, a bad real estate deal can become a good real estate deal. Likewise, a great real estate deal with bad financing can become a horrible real estate deal. So anyone in real estate is forced to get into finance—loans, money, debt, mortgages. (Chapter 7 shows ways to make money with mortgages.)

Consulting

After you have been investing in real estate for a few years, you become an expert and can actually earn money from others (e.g., bankers, other investors, newcomers) for your consulting. People will ask you questions all the time anyway, so consider developing a stream of income that helps you profit from sharing your advice.

Partnering

Partnering (people with different skills and assets working together to form successful real estate ventures) is another path for making money in real estate. You can partner in almost limitless ways: with money, capital, credit, expertise, repairs, and management. Decide what your skills are and stick to them, but also find partners to fill in areas where you lack expertise.

One of the biggest mistakes people make in any business, especially real estate investing, is trying to do everything themselves. Are you prepared to be a finance expert, a real estate acquisition expert, a contractor, a property manager, an accountant, a bookkeeper, and an eviction agent? Are you an attorney or an appraiser? You are wise to get to know those who can help.

Managing Real Estate

You can make money in real estate as a manager mainly by managing tenants. In residential or commercial management, managers generally earn a percentage of rents collected and sometimes a percentage of repairs. Alternatively, they can get commissions (anywhere from 3 to 15 percent) for locating tenants, signing leases, negotiating new leases, and signing and leasing property.

Robert's Business Philosophy

Ask yourself why you want to get into real estate investing. Sure, you want to make a lot of money, but real estate investing is more about freedom.

I urge you to follow my business philosophy, which is to do nothing. That is right—nothing. If I have other professionals doing their jobs properly, I can do next to nothing and profit from it.

For instance, you may have money or credit but little time. Why not locate partners to find deals for you; use *their* time and energy and *your* money or credit. What if you do not have money or credit but have lots of time to look for deals? Partner with people who have money or credit. In the same manner, you can partner with a contractor for your rehabilitation projects or with a management company that manages the rental properties it finds for you.

I must warn you, managing properties requires a tremendous amount of detailed work and can be stressful. Unless you do a lot of it, it's not even very profitable. If you enjoy managing people, then do it, by all means. If not, you can always hire a manager, then manage the manager. Use this approach as another source of real estate income.

Tax Liens

Tax liens usually have to be paid off first when a piece of real estate is sold or foreclosed on. The government has the first claim on the property, even above banks or lenders who have financed a mortgage. Tax liens pay good rates of return, so you might want to familiarize yourself with this concept. (See Chapter 4.)

Judgments and Liens

Investors who are active in real estate or landlords who have a lot of tenants will experience times when people owe them money and they have to collect judgments and liens.

To save on expenses, you could learn how to collect your own judgments and liens. To create another avenue of income, you could take it a step further. Here's how it works. If someone owes $50,000 on his or her property, a judge has put a lien on it, and it hasn't been collected on for five years, you could possibly negotiate the option or the contract to buy that property for $5,000, which is the amount of the judgment. You would approach the owner and say, "Look, you owe $50,000 on this house, but if you pay us $15,000 next week, we'll wipe out the remaining debt. We'll forgive it, forget it, extinguish it." If you did that, you could earn more than $10,000.

Foreclosures

One of the most popular sources of income in real estate is foreclosures. When a house is foreclosed on, it means that a homeowner has borrowed money that he or she cannot repay. The lender takes possession of the property, but in most cases the lender is really interested in recouping the loan's principal balance and expenses incurred.

If a property is worth $100,000 and the principal balance plus expenses due the lender is $100,000, stay away from that deal! However, if that property is worth $162,000 and the lender only wants $100,000 to cover costs, I suggest that you get control of that foreclosure and find out how to profit from it.

You can go to a number of places to find out about foreclosure deals: banks, mortgage companies, government agencies, private lenders, and tax agencies. Remember, though, real estate investors are not out to take advantage of anyone. If you cannot help the person being foreclosed, you do not want to get involved. You are not in the business to get people to sign over houses they do not want to sign over. That would be a bad deal—you never want to get involved in one.

Title and Escrow Closing Fees

Some savvy real estate investors and Realtors have started generating income from title and escrow closing fees. When they get involved in numerous closings, they can make legal and ethical agreements to get marketing or consulting fees for their efforts. Investors might even be able to use another company's computers or office space in exchange for bringing customers on board. This often-overlooked source of income can add significantly to your fountain of wealth.

Buying and Selling Discounted Notes

When you buy (or broker at a discount) a note, you give those people holding notes on properties the opportunity to get their money without waiting the full term of the loan. You might know someone who made arrangements to sell his or her house for $100,000 and took back an $80,000 mortgage. At 30 years at 10 percent interest, he or she may be making $700 a month on that note, with 25 years left to pay. Here is what you say: "Instead of waiting another 25 years to get the rest of your $80,000, how would you like $60,000 in cash in the next few weeks?" Someone needing funds might go for that offer immediately.

A number of people make money by buying notes, so why not make some sales commissions by bringing together buyers and sellers of those notes?

Maintenance and Repair

Owning real estate inevitably involves repairing and maintaining property. If you regularly contract for lawn care, roofing, new appliances, and carpet cleaning and installers, you know which companies provide good prices and service. You are probably willing to recommend those companies to your associates, but it makes sense to make money by setting up a system of referral fees first.

Generally, before I refer a good contractor or maintenance person, I make a contractual agreement that guarantees me from 10 to 20 percent of the bid for a job. Because I am providing work that person would not have had without me, I should earn a commission for that service.

Legal Services

If you are in any business in the United States, especially real estate, you are going to need attorneys. Using prepaid legal services, you can profit from other people needing attorneys by participating in a national legal referral system. By selling prepaid legal expense plans, you can develop another source of income.

Appraisals

Generally, any time a property purchase is being financed by a loan, it needs to be appraised. You could become a professional appraiser—provided you are careful about conflict of interest. Also, you might refer appraisers and, when it is legal and ethical, earn commissions from those referrals.

Insurance

Never buy property without proper insurance, which may include title insurance, liability insurance, fire insurance, and insurance plans specific to commercial property. Someone has to broker and make commissions from all that insurance. Perhaps you could get an insurance license or develop a marketing and referral system with certain trusted agents. That will lead to still another avenue of real estate–related income.

Ancillary Services and Profit Centers

Ancillary services are part of buying, fixing up, and renting property. They can include furniture rental, cable TV rental, Internet service, tenant services, even restaurants. You could generate different forms of income from all of these services by charging referral fees for anything your tenants or clients could possibly need.

For example, if your tenants and clients need a satellite or computer hookup, a moving service, a rental truck, or whatever, you would likely refer them to service providers you know; you might as well get paid for it. You will learn more about these various sources of real estate income in the chapters that follow.

CHAPTER 2

Vision is the art of seeing the invisible.
—JONATHAN SWIFT

Putting *You* into Real Estate Deals

Before we get into the actual mechanics of finding deals, analyzing them, and making money off of them, let us talk about *you*. Every one of you is absolutely different. You have different skills, different assets, different worries, and different goals. You need to decide what you really want to do, how much you really want to make, what you are good at, what you are not good at, what you are scared of, what you are not scared of, and what you feel comfortable with, then start developing a business plan. Whether you are going to own 1 piece of property or 1,000, you are going to have a business. Every business needs a plan. Every business needs goals. Every business needs to decide who its key people are.

If you start a computer company, you do not hire people who are good at raising horses. If you need sales, you do not find people who do not like to talk to people. Likewise, if you go into real estate investing, you want to assign yourself the jobs you are good at, the ones that inspire you.

"Know Thyself"

Write down the real estate activities that are attractive to you. Maybe you love to talk to people and sell things; you will likely be good at getting tenants, putting deals together, and selling the deals. Perhaps you love detail and finance; you would be excellent at doing mortgages and financing deals, but not good at selling them. If you become irritated when people talk to you, you probably do not want to manage property.

Like Socrates said, "Know thyself." Early in my business, I learned quickly what I am not good at—accounting. I stashed receipts in shoeboxes for the first nine months of the year. The other three months, I tried to figure out what I did the first nine months. I used to balance my checkbook by calling up the bank and asking what my balance was. That is no way to run a business. I now have a service that takes care of my bookkeeping and accounting, activities that stress me out today. My checkbook balances, and I know exactly where my financials are. This leaves me free to do what I love—finding and putting deals together.

What do you like to do? What kind of people do you like to be around? What kind of deals would fit your personality? What aspects of real estate investing fit you best? Conversely, what do you *not* like to do? Determine that and partner with someone who does what you hate to do.

This may sound too touchy-feely, but it is important because you do not want to buy property and then agonize because you don't like doing repairs, working with contractors, or dealing with tenants.

Questions to Answer for Yourself

- What do I really like to do?
- What in real estate is attractive to me?
- What do I believe I am best suited for?
- What do I absolutely *not* want to do in real estate (e.g., finding deals, putting in offers, analyzing deals, financing deals, getting partners, selling deals, managing tenants, doing repairs, bookkeeping, making cold calls, looking at properties, talking to a lot of potential buyers, talking to a lot of potential renters, talking to a lot of potential sellers, talking to investors, finding money, borrowing money, legalities, contracts, writing contracts, writing leases)?

Forming Your Team

Whatever aspect of real estate investing you get into, you need a team. You can build your board of directors or your team starting now. To whom do you go when you have finance questions? Legal questions? Contract or repair questions? Whom do you call when you have deals to sell? Start now by asking, "Whom do I want on my team?"

Writing Your Plan

When most real estate investors start out, they have one goal: to get one property. However, they have absolutely no plan. They set out to find that property and, after they buy it, they figure out what to do by accident. When tenants do not pay the rent, for example, they react quickly to evict them without researching alternatives.

Let me save you a lot of time and headache by insisting that you write a plan. Remember the famous study about Yale graduates: It determined that the 3 percent of those graduates who wrote down their goals for the future financially outperformed the other 97 percent three to five times.

Make More Offers

A gentleman named Hal lives in my town, owns a lot more property, and makes a lot more money than I do. Another gentleman named John in Ohio owns more than 900 properties, and he makes a lot more money than Hal. Why is this? Here is the secret: Hal makes more offers than I do, and John makes more offers than Hal. If you never make an offer on a property, you will never get one. I promise that if you make enough offers, some of them—not all of them—will be accepted. Therefore, if you are not happy with how much property or income you are generating from your real estate business, the solution is simple: Make more offers.

I challenge you to, in the next 48 hours, sit down with your loved ones and write out your goals. Decide what you want to have for your 30-day plan, followed by your 60- and 90-day plans, your 6-month plan, and your 1-, 5-, 10-, and 20-year plans. Schedule a couple of hours to record these goals and structure your plans. Remember, your plan does not have to be very long—I suggest between two and six pages. It should include the following items:

- How much property you want to have (in each time frame)?
- What type of activities you want to be involved in?
- How much money you want to make (in each time frame)?
- How much net worth you want to develop?

Most important, write down how you will reach each of your goals—your plan of action. How many phone calls will you make? How many properties will you look at? It is one thing to say, "I would like $10 million worth of real estate," but it means nothing if you do not say how you will get there.

Planning Your Perfect Day at Work

Tie your goals into creating a perfect day at work. How would your perfect day go? Would you have a big office, or a little one?

Would you work out of your home? Where would it be located—in a city, on the beach, or in the mountains?

Beyond the physical setup, determine the nature of your business. What kind of deals would you make? What would your portfolio look like? How much money could you make that day? What would you do to bring in money? Who would you work with?

I planned my perfect day at work a few years ago in Nashville, Tennessee. I saw myself by the beach. I would wake up and exercise, ride around, take some phone calls, do some deals, have lunch, rest in the afternoon or go to the swimming pool, check my messages, do more work in the afternoon, put some deals together, and go out at night or spend time with my family and friends. I would also travel a lot.

I made that plan when I lived in a half-room office in Nashville. Today, I live in a beautiful condominium apartment overlooking downtown Miami and the beach. I ride my scooter and my bicycle around. I wake up early to work out or do yoga on the beach. I come home, check messages, make some phone calls, listen to a few angry tenant requests on voice mail, go to lunch, work some in the afternoon, hang out, and travel a lot. Most of my days are just as I pictured.

Planning Your Perfect Day at Play

Besides your real estate goals, be sure to make overall financial goals, personal goals, family goals, and spiritual goals. How much vacation do you want to have? How much time do you want to spend with your loved ones? How do you want to relax?

When you know this, you can plan your perfect day of play. Write down what that perfect day looks like. Where are you going to be? What are you doing? Who are you with? When you make that first wholesale deal or do a lease option or buy, fix up, and sell a property, reward yourself. Take a small percentage of your profit and get that perfect day of play under way. Maybe you want to take a balloon ride, go on a picnic, go to the mountains, go to the beach, or go on a cruise ship—whatever it is, first set your goals by writing them down.

> *If you do not have the energy to write down your goals, I can assure you that you won't have the energy to make your real estate deals happen.*

Let me give you an example. At a workshop, one of the participants came up to me and said, "Robert, I am going to learn this stuff. All I want to do is make $6,000 and pay off my credit card bill. That is my goal." He went out, flipped one property, earned $6,200, and paid off his Visa bill. He met his goal. He was thrilled.

Another student said, "Robert, I have a lot of overhead. I used to be a corporate executive making a lot of money. I need to make $20,000 a month, no less." He wrote that down as his goal. To make that amount, we agreed that he would have to do a couple of flips a month, buy rental property, broker mortgages, and get active. He really likes doing these activities and now makes between $20,000 and $30,000 a month, just as he pictured.

Your Money and Your Credit

My parents, who brought me up well, always said, "Do not ever talk about money, sex, religion, or credit." I love to talk about all of these things because I find them fascinating; most people do not. However, if you are going to be a successful real estate investor with various income sources, you *do* need to talk about money and credit. You need to get them under control, or at least get started on them. Most real estate investors who have been supersuccessful have also been superbroke.

Start by taking a financial snapshot of where you are today. How much cash do you have? How much credit? What is your credit score? Requesting a copy of your credit report and obtaining a financial statement from a bank or mortgage company will help you to determine what you want to do with your real estate investing as you put these activities into practice. Six months or a year from now, you can compare your snapshot then with now. Realize that you have to know where you are today to be able to get to where you want to be tomorrow.

If you take time now to answer the following questions, you will have a much better idea of what you want to get into. In addition, you will avoid a lot of headaches and frustrations that most investors never take the time to think about.

- How much can you borrow (if you need to) to make real estate investments?
- How much access to cash do you have?
- What are your assets?
- What do you own? (Houses? Cars? Investments?)
- What are your liabilities?
- What are your debts? (Mortgages? Credit cards?)
- How much is your life insurance? Your retirement account?

Take the next two days, the next 48 hours, to make a plan. Decide where you are and where you want to be. Write down your goals and share them with others. You are on your way to developing numerous sources of real estate income.

CHAPTER 3

To win without risk is to triumph without glory.
—**PIERRE CORNEILLE,** *LE CID,* 1636

All Types of Real Estate: Their Advantages and Disadvantages

New real estate investors always ask me what type of real estate is best: land, houses, duplexes, and so on. Should they get into high-end property? Low-end property? Middle-income property? Commercial property? Apartment buildings?

My advice is to pursue whatever you are interested in. Do not ever listen to someone who says, "Only do this type of real estate. Only get into houses. Never do commercial. Only do commercial. Do not do houses. Big apartment buildings are better than little apartment buildings. Trailer parks are the best, better than houses." The truth is it all can work.

Your job is to find a good deal in real estate, whether it is a $3,000 trailer, a $30,000 house, a $300,000 luxury home, a $3 million apartment building, or a $30 million commercial property. Find properties you are comfortable and familiar with at first, then expand. This chapter gives you an overview of different types of investing, so you can consider the advantages and disadvantages of getting into them.

Rental Property

Rentals can be an excellent wealth builder. You buy and hold properties, pay off the debt, and watch the value appreciate. Rentals give you some tax advantages, too. Here are some of your choices.

Trailers and Weekly Rentals

I know some people who will not rent anything if they cannot wheel it around. When I got started in real estate, I would buy a house or duplex for $50,000 in Tennessee and rent it for maybe $700 or $800 a month, at the same time paying off a note of $400 or $500 a month. I was making $200 to $400 every month. For $4,000, my friends would buy a trailer that was 10 or 15 years old. They would fix it up and rent it for $100 or $150 a week. They recovered their initial investment in eight months or less and earned $500 or $600 a month in rent after that. In these two examples, which deal is better? The last one is . . . on paper. However, as with anything, there are advantages and disadvantages.

Advantages

- The cash flow is great.
- The amount you have to invest to get started is minimal.
- The return that you get on your cash flow is good.

Disadvantages

- You deal with a lot of management hassles, transitions, and turnovers.
- You will spend money to keep the cash coming in.

Analyze the situation well, and make sure you count your time and money so you can make a good return on your investment.

Single-Family Homes

What about basic, single-family bread-and-butter homes rented to low- and moderate-income families? You do not need to have a lot of money to get into them; you can leverage out of them; you can buy them for less than what they are worth. They are in high demand, so they are fairly easy to rent and sell if you take care of them.

Advantages

- They are easy to rent.
- They are easy to sell.
- They appreciate fairly nicely.

Disadvantages

- If you own a little house here and a little house there on scattered sites, they are management-intensive.
- If your tenants are low- and moderate-income (or at any level of income) and you do not screen them well, you may face plenty of repairs when they move out.

Condominiums

Renting condominiums has advantages and disadvantages too.

Advantages

- Condominiums are fairly easy to rent. Sometimes they are easy to sell, but not as easy as single-family homes.
- Condominium owners are only responsible for the interior; common areas are kept up by the management association.

Disadvantages

- Condominiums have maintenance and management fees that range from $60 to $300 a month to cover insurance and upkeep of common areas. These sometimes eat into your cash flow.

- The condo association needs to be well funded and not facing any big expenses like a new roof or parking lot. Always do your research first.

Duplexes, Triplexes, and Quadruplexes

Here are some pros and cons of renting duplexes, triplexes, and quadruplexes.

Advantages

- They are easy to finance most of the time because they are deemed residential real estate. This means that anything with fewer than four units can be financed through a residential loan, so they are easier to finance. Remember, properties that are easy to finance are easy to buy and sell.
- They have more than one unit bringing in rent, which helps the cash flow.
- They are fairly easy to rent because people would rather live with just 1 or 2 neighbors than with 400 in a large apartment building.

Disadvantages

- They are harder to sell than houses in a slow market. Single-family, three-bedroom homes are the easiest group to sell.
- They are harder to finance than single-family homes.
- Their biggest disadvantage is also one of their advantages: Because more people are paying rent, collecting rent becomes complicated. Rent-paying situations create more turnover, more repairs, more phone calls, and more management headaches.

Small Apartment Buildings

Smaller apartment buildings, containing between 5 and 100 units, are part of a fragmented market. A lot of mom-and-pop owner-operators run small apartment buildings.

A Rose by Another Name

In certain areas of the United States, duplexes are called *doubles*, triplexes are called *triples*, and quadruplexes are called *fourplexes*. In my opinion, it doesn't matter what you call them if they make money for you.

Advantages

- You receive great cash flow.

- You can usually hire an on-site manager to take care of things because all of the tenants live in one place and are not scattered.

- You can have economies of scale because all of the apartments are in one place.

Disadvantages

- As the number of units goes up, vacancy and repair rates go up, which translate into more turnover, more repairs, more people, and more headaches.

- It is harder to sell an apartment building than a home if the market goes bad because it is an investment property.

- It is more difficult to find financing for an apartment building than for a home. Rarely will a bank or mortgage company loan more than between 60 and 80 percent of the purchase price of a small apartment building.

Large Apartment Buildings

Large apartment complexes are usually run by large organizations. This market requires a lot of capital and can be very competitive.

Advantages

- Large apartment buildings provide economies of scale.

- Large apartment buildings are easy to manage with all tenants in one place. Finding great deals on apartment buildings becomes more competitive with 100- to 200-unit complexes because many large commercial companies invest in these.

Then you may be competing against large real estate companies and institutions with tremendous amounts of capital. However, many real estate investors profit well from the smaller complexes that have from 10 to 50 units.

Disadvantages

- They can be hard to finance because of size.
- They can be tough to sell in a down market.

Commercial Property

Commercial property here refers to strip centers, office buildings, and commercial warehouses.

Advantages

- The tenants generally take care of all the repairs, unlike in residential properties.
- The rents can be lucrative, especially for big spaces.

Disadvantages

- Commercial property is more difficult to finance than residential property.
- Commercial property often requires time to find another tenant that suits the space. This means that you have to be willing to pay the note or pay the costs, taxes, and insurance while the space becomes rented and retooled for a new tenant.
- Commercial property stays empty longer than residential property when the economy is down.

Land Developments

Land developments involve investors finding land, getting it under control, improving it with roads or utilities, then selling it for a big profit, either through a residential developer or a commercial developer. It is a great business.

What Options Suit You Best

Your main job in developing unlimited riches in real estate is to find good deals. Once you learn the tools (e.g., for wholesaling and lease optioning), it does not matter whether the property is a piece of land, a house, a duplex, or a giant apartment building. Use the methods in this book to learn what options suit you best.

One of my favorite sayings: The two best businesses in the world are buying whiskey by the bottle and selling it by the shot, and buying land by the acre and selling it by the lot.

Advantages

- A land development gives you the potential for a tremendous profit because you are dealing with a bigger chunk of land.
- A land development will likely increase in value, especially if you improve it with roads and services.

Disadvantages

- You have to have *real* money because the land does not produce any income.
- You have costs (e.g., mortgage, taxes, insurance) while you are holding the land.
- You can sell land easily in prosperous times; however, in hard times, you may have difficulty selling it.

CHAPTER 4

Patience, persistence and perspiration make an unbeatable combination for success.
—NAPOLEAN HILL

Every Possible Way to Find Great Deals in Real Estate

This book shows you how to analyze deals; contract deals; lease option deals; wholesale property; buy, fix up, and sell property; rent property; and determine many other possible avenues of income you can get from real estate investing. However, one critical detail must be covered first: how to find a good deal.

If you cannot find a good deal in real estate, you cannot make any money. You cannot develop all of those sources of income without finding good deals. (Unfortunately, this is the critical part that a lot of books, seminars, and conferences about real estate leave out.)

What Is a Great Deal?

Let's say a friend of yours is getting divorced, has to move away, needs cash quickly, and says, "I have this Jaguar worth about $50,000. It's in great shape. If I could just get $30,000 for it, I'd be okay." The car was brand new the year before, purchased for about $55,000.

Could you figure out a way to make money off that Jaguar? You could call dealers, who are wholesalers, and ask, "What is a 2001 Jaguar worth today?" They might reply, "About $50,000." So you would ask, "What would you pay for it?" and they might say, "We'd have to make something on the resale, so we'd pay $42,000 for it."

If the dealership gave you $42,000 and you gave your friend $30,000, you would make $12,000. Alternatively, you could run an ad in the newspaper offering the Jaguar for, say, $45,000. You would make even more money. Or you could take $30,000 from your savings or borrow from a bank, lease the Jaguar for $600 a month, and bring in money every month for it.

You have these choices in real estate, too, but first you have to find a good deal like your friend with the Jaguar handed you. If you find a good deal, you will make good money. If you find a great deal, you will make great money.

Finding Motivated Sellers

To find good deals, find motivated sellers. If a property is worth $100,000 in the marketplace and the seller wants $99,000 for it, the seller simply is not hungry to sell. So what motivates some people to sell at below-market prices and how can you identify them?

Let me give you an example. I once called about a house after seeing a newspaper ad that stated "Must Sell." I called the gentleman

What Is One Deal Worth?

What if you find that great deal—a house you can turn over, flip, or wholesale? You make $8,000, or $12,000, or $20,000 in a short time by selling it shortly after you buy it. What is one deal worth to you? (See Chapter 7.)

What if you find one great deal—a house you could buy and hold? You borrow $100,000, rent the house out, and pay for it in 15 years. By then, it is worth $300,000 and you have made thousands on it. (See Chapter 7.)

What if you lease-option a house? With this method, you get three paydays. The tenants pay you up front with option money. You lease it out every month and make $300 to $500 extra cash flow coming in every month. And when they actually buy the house, you make another $15,000. (See Chapter 8.)

Returns like these are possible with good and great deals. If you are not searching out these deals, you could be wasting your time in real estate.

who placed the ad and he said, "It's a five-bedroom, three-bath, with a pool and tennis court in a great neighborhood." I knew that house had to be worth $400,000 to $500,000 because I was familiar with this neighborhood in Nashville, Tennessee.

I asked, "Is it in good shape?"
"It's in perfect shape," he replied.
"What do you want for your house?"
"I want one dollar." Was he motivated to sell? Yes.

I generally do not try to figure out why people do what they do, but I asked him, "Why are you selling it for a dollar?" He answered, "I'm getting divorced and I've got to split the assets with my wife. I can't wait to give her fifty cents." What was his motivation? Revenge. I had no desire to know more about their relationship. It was none of my business. But I did want to buy this home for a dollar.

Unfortunately, the judge in divorce court would not approve the contract (which I wrote under the seller's guidance) to buy the house for a dollar. The judge threw it out, but I got the house for a lot less than it was worth (though it was more than a dollar).

Here are some additional indicators for identifying highly motivated sellers.

- Poor health
- Divorce
- Unemployment
- Estate sales due to death
- Moving on to a new location or a new lifestyle

Sometimes people face a health crisis, a divorce, or the death of a loved one. They lose their jobs or their desire to care for their property. Through their transitions, they have difficulty paying

Stop Trying to Understand Why

If you follow this advice, you will save a lot of time, headaches, and psychic energy in real estate investing.

Stop trying to figure out why people do what they do.

Why do people smoke? They know it is going to kill them. Why do people not go to the gym? Why do they not take care of their health? Why do they not donate money to charity? Why isn't everybody happy? Why do people spend ridiculous amounts of money on ridiculous things?

This book is not about teaching psychology. If you are reading it, you want to be a successful real estate investor, not a counselor. Your job is to find good deals, not to understand why people do what they do. However, it is wise to find out the circumstances people face. Their life events certainly affect their motivation to sell at below-market pricing.

their expenses, including their mortgages. Although the circumstances may be sad, if you can help them prevent foreclosing on their property by getting cash into their hands, you have done them a service.

Please realize I am not saying to take advantage or rip people off. If you ever have a transaction in which every party is not completely satisfied with the deal, move on.

You can experiment with a variety of ways to find sellers, including going through newspapers and brokers. Be sure to use these approaches consistently so you know which ones work best for you.

Reading Newspaper Ads

I got started in this business Sunday mornings while enjoying my favorite hot drink at home and reading the newspaper. About half of all the deals I have ever found, even the great ones, have come from newspaper ads. Calling on ads at least every Sunday or more often will get you started. If you follow sports, you read the Sunday paper religiously. You learn about the heights and weights of the athletes, their playing statistics, even their arrest records in some cases. If you study the real estate section in the same way, you will become an expert in real estate like you are in sports. It is similar to how some people follow stocks. They know every detail about them and watch their movements 15 times a day. If you did one-tenth of that activity in real estate by steadily going to the real estate section every week, you would become an expert in real estate.

When you read the newspaper, what are you looking for? Suspects—highly motivated sellers who become prospects. The following nine ideas suggest where to look to get started.

For Rent Ads

If a property is for rent, it is often empty and the owners have a mortgage on it but are not collecting rent. The landlord or management company may be tired of renting it out and keeping it repaired. Sometimes you can get some great deals and help the owner get out of the business altogether.

For Sale by Owner Ads

If people are selling their houses by themselves, that might mean they cannot afford a Realtor, do not want to get a Realtor, or are in a hurry to sell.

For Sale Ads

Look at For Sale ads to quickly learn what property sells for in specific neighborhoods. Search for phrases such as "Must Sell," "Make Offer," and "Won't Last." I circle those ads and call to find suspects who might become prospects.

In the process of calling, you will learn which Realtors are active in those areas. Get to know them because if you ever find a deal in their territory, they could help you locate buyers or sellers.

"Must Sell"

A student of mine, Don, saw a "Must Sell" ad in the newspaper for a commercial property in Miami, Florida. He did not know much about Miami, but he called the broker listed in the ad and asked this critical question: "Why are you selling?" The broker replied, "The woman is selling because her husband was the landlord. He just passed away and she doesn't want to manage it. She's tired of it. She wants to dump it. The building is worth as much as $1.4 million but it needs $200,000 of work. She'd take $500,000 for it." Don offered a lot less than that and got the building under contract for $290,000. He wants to wholesale it and stands to make between $100,000 and $300,000. The end buyer will also get a great deal because Don is asking $700,000 to $800,000 for this $1.4 million building.

Who wins? Everybody. The widow is happy to let go of the property after making money with it over the last 30 years. The broker will make a good commission; Don will see a large profit; the end buyer will get an incredible deal. And it all started from answering an ad in the local newspaper.

Investment Property Ads

I like to call ads under the heading "Investment Properties" because I know investors own these properties being advertised. An investor or landlord has either purchased a property years ago and wants the profits from the appreciation in value, or has bought a bad deal and is tired of messing with the property. In both cases, the owner could be highly motivated to sell.

When I call, I always ask, "Do you have or know of any other properties for sale?" I recommend always asking that question when you call. Here is why.

I once responded to an ad from this section and the older gentleman who answered said, "I've got this property and I'm selling it at 30 percent below what it's worth. I'll do owner's terms. I have pictures of it and I really want to sell, so I'll be more than glad to work with you." Then I asked that important question. "Do you have any others?" He said, "I'm so glad you asked. I've got 88 more, all with pictures and documentation." I ended up buying all of them and flipped about 50 in about a year.

Lease-Option Ads

Check for a Lease-Option section in your paper. Investors looking for deals or putting deals together usually place ads here. Remember, they are investors. And if you are also an investor who is going to be wholesaling, you not only want deals that you can buy but you want people you can sell to. Always get their names, addresses, phone numbers, fax numbers, e-mail addresses, and what type of property they like. Another critical question to ask is: "Do you know of any good sources of financing?" Build your lists of people who can get you money as well as get you deals.

Every time you talk to an investor, you are looking for three things:

1. A deal *you* can buy
2. A deal of yours that *they* can buy
3. Good sources of financing

Auction Ads

Auctions, listed in the back of the real estate section, are becoming a popular way to sell property. Some estimate that in the next five years, about 40 to 50 percent of all property may be auctioned.

Auction companies advertise, conduct the auction, sell the property, and close the deal 10 to 30 days later. If they have deals they cannot auction, they sell them at a discount because auctioneers are always finding motivated sellers who want to off-load their properties quickly.

When you go to real estate auctions, whom do you meet? Buyers who have cash. (Some deals offer owner's terms or financing, but many require cash.) So go to an auction as if it were a cocktail party. Meet everybody there and build your list of buyers. Get names, addresses, phone numbers, e-mail addresses, and fax numbers. These investors find deals that they could pass on to you, and vice versa. All the while, you keep your eyes open for a great deal.

Legal Notices

You will find legal notices in many newspapers. They announce bankruptcies, divorces, foreclosures, and estate sales. You might find highly motivated sellers in any one of these areas, plus you can find a lot of great deals and work with your attorney on the technical details. These deals can be worth the effort.

Every major city has a legal newspaper. Call a local attorney or go to a magazine shop, find out the name, and buy it. It is full of foreclosures, tax liens, bankruptcies, estate sales, and divorces. You do not have to understand the legal mumbo jumbo. You simply call the attorney listed or get an address off the legal notice and send a letter asking about suspects for good deals.

Obituaries

If an obituary is in the newspaper, what does that mean to you? The deceased usually leaves behind real estate, furniture, cars, and

Get to Know Law Firms in Your Town

Generally, in any given town, a couple of top law firms handle most of the foreclosures and bankruptcies. Get to know the people in those firms and work with them. Understand that they care about client confidentiality, so they cannot tell you certain things, but they do know about pending deals. They will call somebody about them, so it might as well be you.

often family members who live all over. You could be doing their relatives a service by writing or calling them and saying, "I am so sorry to hear about your loss, but if you have any property you want to dispose of quickly, I can help you. I might be interested in taking it over." In a lot of instances, people say, "We don't want to mess with this house. The children and cousins have moved across the country. Just take the house; you're doing us a favor. Yes, we know we're selling way below what it is worth, but we don't have time to deal with it. Too many memories. Just take it."

I have been teaching this method for years and one of my students has been extremely successful. He responds to all the obituaries in writing and usually gets about 10 to 20 deals a year in a very small town. Many times, the people write him a letter thanking him after he has put the property under contract, flipped it, fixed it up, and sold it. They say, "Thank you so much for taking that property off our hands. We didn't want to have to deal with everything." So sometimes he not only gets the houses, but also acquires cars, furniture, and collectibles.

Neighborhood Newspapers

Some of the best deals can be found in the *Thrifty Nickel,* the *Shopper's News,* and other neighborhood papers because people who place ads there cannot afford to advertise in the big paper. I have experimented and found that if you have $200 to advertise with, you will likely get better results from advertising in the smaller papers. Not only are they good sources for finding deals, but you also get more bang for your buck in advertising. (More about advertising later in this chapter.)

Driving for Dollars

Driving for dollars. Doesn't it sound like a game show? "Good evening, ladies and gentlemen. In tonight's edition of *Driving for Dollars,* we have two contestants." But you can make a lot of money at this game, which is my favorite way of finding good deals. It is fun to go with someone who will write down the addresses as you find promising properties.

Pick a neighborhood that you are interested in: one that is in transition, is being fixed up, has houses that need work, and so on. Drive around it slowly and try to find at least 20 addresses you can write down for neglected, vacant, or condemned homes, ones with signs saying For Sale, For Sale by Owner, or For Rent.

Be persistent. You may have to call and call and call to find the owners. Start by calling the Registrar of Deeds, getting on the Internet, and going to the local tax records office to locate the owners. Ask a Realtor friend to look them up on the MLS computer. Then call or write to the owners once you find them.

As you drive around, how do you tell if a house might be owned by a motivated seller? Look for the following characteristics.

Neglect

Needy homes have gutters that hang, roofs with holes in them, and horrible-looking yards with trash lying everywhere. A general rule in real estate is this: The worse disrepair, the better the deal. As an investor, begin to love houses that have black goo dripping out of the ceiling, animal dung on the carpet, holes in the wall, broken windows, and 14 feet of garbage in the yard. The more work the house needs, the more motivated the seller will be. The more motivated the seller, the better the deal will be.

The best deal my friend John ever got involved a house that had 35 feet of garbage in the front yard. Drug addicts had lived in it. When he walked into the house, he could not even get access to the basement because of the garbage.

But the real estate market was hot in this neighborhood and 50 people looked at the house during its first two days on the market. Everybody who saw it walked away in disgust. Most people insist on buying a house that looks like a new present with a bow on it.

So John went into the trashed-out house, took a big breath in the smelly environment, and declared, "Ah, Paradise. Eureka. The mother lode." He figured that house was worth about $350,000 fixed up. He determined it needed about $50,000 of repair. So he put it under contract for $140,000 (less than half of its value) and got the deal done. This example proves my point: The worse the house, the better the deal.

Undeveloped Land

My friend Bill, an investor in Nashville, Tennessee, finds big chunks of land—20 acres, 50 acres, 200 acres—negotiates the price, and puts the land under contract. I asked Bill, "Where do you find most of these deals?" He said, "I drive around, find land on the edge of town, and either talk to the neighbors or write a letter and find the owner. I have never used a Realtor because the property is rarely listed."

Bill finds owners, asks if they would like to sell their land, and gets an option to buy it. If it is unimproved farmland, he reads the property codes for that area and often gets the land rezoned to make it more attractive to future buyers. He might borrow money from a partner or from the bank, then puts in roads and utilities to increase the land's value immediately. Three months to two years later, he sells this land (under option at $800,000) for $1.5 million to $3 million. You can do that, too.

Vacant Homes

If houses are empty, the grass is high, the bushes are overgrown, and the properties look deserted, could those sellers be motivated? Absolutely. Put them on your list of suspects.

Condemned Homes

Look for that yellow tape that says, "Unfit for human habitation." This signifies a code violation. That is exciting for investors because owners who have already been to court might be highly motivated to sell. The codes enforcement area of the Housing Administration has fined them. The fines are equivalent to saying, "If you do not fix this house, we will fine you more, and if you still don't fix it by a certain time, we will bulldoze your property."

Some condemned homes require a tremendous amount of work to fix up, maybe too much. The windows could be broken and the electricity or the heat may not work. You always have to ask if it is a good investment.

Not only can you spot these "diamonds in the rough" while driving for dollars, you can access a list of addresses for condemned homes posted by the Housing Administration.

For Rent Signs

If a house is for rent, you might locate a highly motivated landlord who bought the property 20 years ago for one-fifth of what it is worth today and is tired of it. The best ones are the empty ones. Call about these, too.

For Sale and For Sale by Owner Signs

As you drive for dollars, look for For Sale and For Sale by Owner signs. Some of these signs might say, "Make Offer," so pay close attention. Because you are still driving neighborhoods, learning about the neighborhoods, and getting suspects, make a point of meeting the Realtors and brokers who are active in that area. You will learn a tremendous amount from talking with them and from carefully reading the signs.

The Smaller the Sign, the Better the Deal

Mary, a student of mine, was once driving around (you have to go really slow when you are driving for dollars) and almost missed a little bitty sign behind a bush. She got out of her car, jumped over a low fence, moved the bush, and saw one of those little For Sale signs available for 90 cents at the hardware store. She could hardly even read the phone number. In fact, she wrote down eight different phone numbers she thought it might be, and found the seventh one to be correct. On the phone call, she asked the man who answered, "How long has your house been for sale?" He replied, "Six months. You're the first caller." How would you like to be a market of one? Mary bought that house for about half of what it was worth, wholesaled it, and made about $20,000.

She also asked that magic question, "Do you have any others?" He replied, "Yes, I have another one. It's a few blocks away. No one has called about that one either." She drove by that house and saw the sign there had completely fallen off. She was able to make a good deal on that house, too.

Auctions

In addition to the auctions listed in the newspaper, look for other auction companies in the Yellow Pages. When you drive around for dollars, you will see signs about upcoming auctions. Call all of the auction companies and **get on their announcement lists,** so whenever they do an auction, they send you a notice for auctions of a commercial property, house, apartment building, land, and so on. Attend all of those auctions that have properties; you might find a great deal.

Locating Owners

What if you can't find owners? One investor was driving for dollars and found some vacant homes, wrote the addresses down, went to the Internet, and looked on the tax rolls, but still could not find the owners.

It is almost always certain that *someone* almost always owns a property, whether it is an individual, a corporation, or an estate.

There is a name on a title at the tax records; it might even belong to someone who died 10 years ago. Or it might have been a factor in some kind of lawsuit. To find out what happened to the title, hire a title searcher and get the names of people listed, then locate them.

You could also hire a private investigator. For between $100 and $500, private investigators can find owners and probably learn what happened to the property. (My web site, www.shemin.com, gives names of private investigators we recommend.)

Now, what if no one owns that property and no title exists? Then you go to court, hire an attorney, and file an action to "quiet title." A judge will decide what is necessary to clear up the title or get a good title. Sometimes the judge will ask you or your attorney to advertise and see if anyone has an interest in the property. You will then be required to contact by certified letter anyone who has an interest in the property. This often occurs when there is a death and there is subsequently no proper passing of title.

If you have a problem getting good title for a property, you need to contact a good title attorney who can guide you as to what it will require to clear up the title for a property. This is a very difficult process, though. If no one owns it, it becomes hard to acquire the property. So you have to decide if the deal is potentially worth the work and expense it would take.

Also ask, "What seven or ten numbers can I dial to get the answer?" Personally, I would call my local title lawyer and say, "I have found this property and cannot find the owner. What do you recommend? In our jurisdiction, how do you get proper title?"

Foreclosures

A foreclosure occurs when someone lends another person money to buy property and the money is not paid back. Because the property provides the guarantee for the loan, the lender has the right to take it back, usually through a first, second, or third mortgage or tax lien.

Who lends money? In our country, mostly banks and mortgage companies provide property loans. Some governmental agencies have the authority to get a lien or judgment for nonpayment of funds owed (usually for taxes) and can foreclose on a property.

There are generally two types of foreclosures: (1) a judicial foreclosure, in which a lender has to go to court and get a judge to order the foreclosure, and (2) a deed foreclosure, or deed of trust foreclosure, in which the deed to the property is put in trust after the loan period is over. The unpaid mortgage is advertised for about 30 to 60 days. After that, the attorney or trustee forecloses on the property and takes possession of the deed through the trust.

It does not really matter to which type (judicial or deed of trust) you go. The important part is to understand the technicalities of foreclosure. For example, is the judgment final or is there a right of redemption? (That is, can the homeowner come back within six months or a year and pay off the loan and get the house back? In most states, that is not possible; when they get that property back, they have to pay the lender all the money back plus interest.)

Legal Newspapers

Foreclosure deals are generally listed in the community's legal newspaper. In most cities and counties, foreclosures have to be

Make Sure That the Title Is Good

Can you be sure you will get a good title at the foreclosure sale? On whom do you rely to give you answers? I recommend you work with experts from a reputable title company. Also, get an attorney who understands foreclosures and does research well. You do not have to understand title and foreclosure law; you *do* have to know how to talk to people who can answer those questions for you.

I understand foreclosures; I am an attorney by training. However, before I buy any property, I always get a title search done or consult with my title or escrow company to make sure I am buying what I want to buy.

advertised in the legal or regular papers a few weeks before the sale occurs. You could also call the tax assessor's office or go to the Registrar of Deeds and ask for the list of the properties going into foreclosure.

Foreclosures can be excellent deals. Some people make tons of money. Unfortunately, they come with some disadvantages. For example, often you cannot have access to the property before you buy it because the bank may have sealed it. So you have to make sure you understand the risks when you buy those foreclosures.

Tax Sales

If people do not pay their property taxes, the government taxing entity will demand payment and force a tax foreclosure. You can buy the property at a tax sale, or, in certain states, you can buy a tax certificate for the amount of the back taxes. By using a certificate, you get interest on your money or on the property. Some tax certificates pay anywhere from 10 to 30 percent interest. People buy at tax sales for two reasons:

1. They hope to get the property for the price of back taxes. For example, if a $200,000 property has $8,000 of property taxes not paid and goes to a tax sale, they want to buy it for $8,000, the amount of the back taxes. Of course, others may bid against you and raise the price. Still, you can find good deals at tax sales.

2. Many cities, counties, and states by law demand that the taxes owed and the amount bid collect a good interest rate. In certain areas, every taxing authority has rules and laws for how sales are run. Some require as much as 20 to 30 percent interest paid.

For example, the owner of a house worth $200,000 owes $8,000 in back taxes. You bid $8,000 with the intent to acquire the house for the amount of taxes only. However, your city has a one-year right of redemption rule. This means the homeowner has one year to pay back all of the taxes and interest due and redeem the property. For example, if your area's interest rate for tax liens is 20 percent, then the homeowner pays you $8,000 plus 20 percent to get the house back. If the homeowner does not pay you off within one year, you get to keep the $200,000 home. However, you cannot sell that house until the year is up.

Alternatively, you could get a property for the amount of the tax lien. You can also acquire properties by bidding on them by auction at foreclosure sales. The IRS also puts tax liens on property.

After you hear of a pending tax sale or foreclosure and before it happens is when you should to talk to the property owners affected. Are they motivated to sell? Yes. Are they hard to talk to sometimes? Yes, because people have a psychological defense mechanism called denial. Sometimes people say, "No, I don't want to talk to you. I'm going to win the lottery. Someone will show up at my door and give me a million dollars. I know it's going to happen, so leave me alone."

So they are difficult to talk to, but in most cases, the things that are hardest to obtain are the sweetest. So work these foreclosures and preforeclosure tax sales, and develop a good source of income.

Department of Veterans Affairs

The Department of Veterans Affairs guarantees loans for veterans and publishes a list of houses it is foreclosing on. Sometimes they are good deals and occasionally they offer very favorable financing. Check with mortgage brokers for details about good deals from the Department of Veterans Affairs. (See www.shemin.com for recommendations of government real estate agencies.)

Housing and Urban Development (HUD)

HUD also guarantees loans that banks make. It takes properties back for unpaid mortgages and you can bid on its foreclosed properties. Most real estate brokers and agents have access to lists of

HUD foreclosures in the area. They could be a great place to find deals. (See www.shemin.com for links to HUD lists.)

Questions and Answers

Q: I do not have a Realtor's license. Can I still make money in foreclosures?

A: Yes. You do not need a real estate license in most cases. I have bought and sold a lot of properties. I can put them under contract or option and sell them to somebody else. A real estate license only lets you go to the Multiple Listing Service (MLS) and make commissions off the sales of properties that are listed. This book outlines other creative ways to make money in real estate besides using MLS.

Courts

Some real estate investors always complain about the government: the IRS, courts, regulations. But I love the government. As a real estate investor, you should love the government, too, because it is hard at work making hundreds of thousands of motivated sellers. All types of courts exist to help create motivated sellers (even when they did not think they were motivated). Here are some of them.

Codes Court

Go down to your local housing administration office to find out scheduled dates for codes court, where landlords and investors go to defend their interests. The codes court enforces the codes and can issue fines. It can even condemn homes and have them bull-dozed. Do motivated sellers come to these courtrooms? Yes.

The proceedings are all public record. The docket for the day is usually posted outside of the courthouse. You can talk to the people while they are there and meet with lawyers, landlords, and investors who come. Every time I go to codes court, I usually find a good deal. Chances are you will, too.

Eviction Court

In every major city, evictions go to court at least a few days a week. Who shows up there? Tenants, attorneys, landlords, and managers. Owners who have a conflict on their hands and go to court to resolve it could be in the market to sell for a good price.

Know that when you go to eviction court, you may find some great deals, and you will also find better entertainment than any TV sitcom. You will also network with people you want to know. If you do not want to spend time there, you can get names, addresses, and phone numbers of people on the docket. Send them a letter that asks, "Do you have any properties you'd like to sell?" and follow up.

Environmental Court

People who have too much junk on their properties wind up in this court. It fines people for not removing trash and not cleaning their yards. Owners of these properties can be highly motivated to sell. Go meet them, get their names, and contact them afterward. They could turn into good deals.

Divorce Court

Because divorce records are public, you can actually look up case files and see what a couple owns. Many have a home that they must sell and are often willing to take a discount just to settle the assets to get out of the marriage quickly. Get to know some divorce attorneys and show up at divorce court. You might find some good suspects there.

Estate and Probate Court

You can look in the public records where deceased persons' assets are listed. Contact the attorneys and the families and say, "Would you like to unload these properties quickly? I can help you out." Do you think you can find some deals that way?

One Good Probate Deal

When the grandparents of a real estate investor I know passed away, they left behind a condominium in Florida. The family members did not want to spend time getting rid of the property and dealing with the memories, so they sold the condo to a gentleman who contacted them through a letter. He got the address from the estate probate record. The condo and other assets sold for about 60 percent of their worth. This gentleman saved the family a lot of trouble and got a great deal in the process.

Advertising

Most real estate investors do not like to tell people what they do. They tend to be laid-back types who drive nondescript cars. If you have a quiet personality, you can get over your shyness through advertising. In my experience, businesses that have a mediocre product or service but advertise a lot bring in plenty of customers. Fast food restaurants are a good example of that—they have poor food and mediocre service, but people spend money there every day because they see the advertisements constantly.

In real estate investing, the more you advertise, the more the word gets out, and the more deals you will get. Here are some inexpensive forms of advertising you can use.

Business Cards

Make your card stand out by printing your information on a shocking-bright paper. The wording on your card should get attention and tell people what you can do for them. "We will pay cash for your house. Can close quickly. Call me first. Call me last." You might include wording like, "If you are in trouble through foreclosure, bankruptcy, divorce, need to raise cash, need to raise money, need to sell your property quickly, call me now." Put your cell phone number on the card in a prominent place. Hand out your cards to everybody.

Flyers

Make flyers—and distribute lots of them. They might say, "We will pay cash for your house. Can close quickly. Call me first. We will buy your house. We will make an offer on every property." You want your phone to ring so you can find great deals.

Ads

Place an ad in your local newspaper that states, "We will buy houses. We will pay cash." Typically, these ads generate two to three calls a day and lead to about one deal a week. Is it worth $190 a week to run an ad? Yes, because one deal can be worth a lot.

Run your ad consistently and for a long time. This is critical. If you run it for three months to a year and the wording attracts attention, you will get calls and, eventually, good deals.

Direct Mail

Sending direct mail through the postal service usually gets a response rate of 1 to 2 percent, so do not expect a high-volume return for your efforts. However, if you mail a large quantity, you will get activity. Monitor the numbers carefully, and be consistent with your direct-mail campaign, so you know which mailings work well for you.

Door Hangers

When you come home at night, sometimes you see hanging on your door advertisements for carpet cleaning and pizza specials. You can use this idea and pay the same people to hand out your door hangers. Your message would read: "We pay cash for a house. Can close quickly. Do you know of any houses for sale that are a good deal? Call me. Referral fees paid."

Signs

Put signs in your targeted neighborhood on every corner and you will get calls. The largest real estate franchises attract their prospects by running billboards that say, "We will buy any house, ugly or pretty. We will pay cash. Call now." These signs generate lots of calls and the companies make tons of money.

Car Signs

I flew to Ohio one time to speak at a real estate association. I noticed the fellow who picked me up at the airport had put a big plastic sign on the side of his Jeep Cherokee that said, "We will pay cash for your house. Call me." I thought, "I don't like the way this ugly sign covers up a beautiful truck." Nonetheless, I asked Dennis if he got calls from this sign. He replied, "I get about five calls a week and one deal a month. I made about $8,000 on one of them last month and $25,000 on a fixer-upper." That ugly sign becomes a beautiful one when motivated sellers call you.

Co-op Advertising

You can partner with businesses that are already advertising through flyers, door hangers, even pizza boxes. Instead of advertising alone, you combine your efforts with others and spread your message farther for the same amount of money and time spent.

Think about all the people advertising on restaurant menus, on shopping carts, on street signs in your targeted neighborhoods. If you can cooperate with any of them, you will generate calls that can lead to deals.

To Advertise or Not to Advertise

My experience is that if you do not advertise, nothing will happen. And if you do advertise, something will happen.

An investor named John in Ohio owns more than 900 houses. Why does he have 900 houses while you and I do not? Because he places signs on park benches, on street corners, on pizza boxes. He prints and distributes flyers, door hangers, and business cards. This kind of advertising works where John is, and it will work where you live, too.

Networking

I once attended a seminar in which I learned some information that will save you lots of time learning it yourself. It is this: When people get into financial trouble—heading for bankruptcy or foreclosure—they follow a predictable pattern of behavior. They run to their accountants, mortgage brokers, and financial planners. In desperation, they may call a Realtor and say, "Can you sell my house in three weeks?" As a last resort, they call a bankruptcy attorney.

Because of this pattern, you want to build a network of mortgage bankers, Realtors, attorneys, and accountants so that when desperate people call, they will send them to you. You can pay them cash for their house, quick-turn it, make money yourself, and possibly stop them from going bankrupt.

Investing is a lonely business. Go meet other people, talk to them, and help each other out. Here are some categories of people who can refer good deals to you.

Real Estate Agents

Real estate agents have access to the MLS and to buyers and sellers. Get to know the active agents in your targeted areas. When

---

Three Steps to Start

What will you do in the next 30 days to get some deals? Here is a three-step formula to follow:

1. Go to three auctions.
2. Make a point of meeting five investors there.
3. Take each of them to lunch and ask how they began, if they have any deals, what they are looking for, who they use for financing, and so on.

Tell them you are getting started and they will love to help you out.

---

good deals come their way, they will call someone, and that someone should be you. Make sure they get paid when they find deals so you keep your relationships golden. By the way, if I use agents and brokers but do not close on a property with them, I give them a check for their time until they find me something. It keeps the relationship solid.

Attorneys

Attorneys do a lot of things that can help your business: estate sales, divorces, bankruptcies. Find several active attorneys in your area and network with them.

CPAs, Accountants, Bookkeepers

When people want to do financial planning, settle their estate, sell some property, raise money, or get out of financial trouble, they turn to their trusted accountant or financial planner. These professionals often help clients dispose of their property, so get to know them and build your network.

Bankers and Mortgage Brokers

Bankers and brokers make loans to real estate people and often know where good deals are. Because they have access to funds, they can possibly finance the good deals you find. They also know lots of other investors and can help you expand your network.

Bird-dogging

Bird dogs are the white dogs with brown spots that flush out rabbits and quails in a hunting situation. In real estate, bird dogs are people who can flush out deals for you.

Most successful businesses rely on many people to get things done, and everyone in the organization benefits. It is hard to be a lone wolf in the investing business; you can only look at so many deals, drive around so many neighborhoods, write so many letters, and make so many phone calls yourself.

Who can act as your bird dogs to spot good deals for you? Everyone you know, because everyone knows someone who has to sell a property at a discount or is dealing with an estate, getting a divorce, having money problems, going into bankruptcy, and so on.

Did you know that if you are a Realtor, it is illegal to pay a finder's fee? But, if you are a real estate investor, you can do what you want within the confines of the law. That means you can pay referral fees. And when you pay people, they keep coming back with more deals.

Following are several categories of people whom you can ask to be your bird dogs.

Contractors

Every contractor, big or small, is going out looking at properties that need work. They know owners and some of those owners will be motivated to sell. So contact every contractor and repair person you know and say, "If you bring me a deal that I close on, I will pay you a finder's fee."

Utility Workers

Utility workers—from the gas company, electric company, or water company—are walking and driving through neighborhoods every day. They know a lot about houses, neighborhoods, and the people with whom they deal. They may be able to say, "Hey, I know about a house that needs a lot of work. We shut the gas or the water off. And here is the owner or the address." Utility workers can be your bird dogs.

Post Office Workers

Often postal workers know more about you and your neighbors than you think they do. They know who is getting divorced, who is moving, who has to sell a house. In fact, some successful real estate investors *are* post office workers. Ask them to help you identify good deals.

Police Officers

Police officers have a tough job in the neighborhoods. They get to know about houses or property that can be sold, especially ones they just locked up because somebody did something naughty in there. They can point you to motivated sellers.

Nursing Home Workers

Our population is getting older and more people are moving into retirement, assisted living, and nursing homes. Often, people are forced to sell their property and their assets to qualify for financial assistance before going into a home.

One of my students hangs out at nursing homes to find good deals. He makes friends with the administrators, who call him and say, "Mrs. Smith has to sell her home, and the family doesn't want to deal with it. Can you help them out?" He gets a lot of good deals that way. He is not taking advantage of the situation; he is truly helping them. He discloses in writing exactly what he is doing.

Three More Ideas

I have found the following three ideas to be among the best ways to find good deals in real estate. Pick any of them, work them consistently, and you will make money.

Call Retail Finance Companies

Located in malls and shopping centers, these companies make high-risk loans to high-risk borrowers. Look them up in the Yellow Pages under finance companies. Some of their names are Associates, Beneficial, and American General. They make all kinds of loans, but also lend money to people who may not have perfect credit. Some will have local, regional, or national foreclosure centers where you can call about properties available. Often, they will sell them for the outstanding amount of the loan.

Write Letters

Whenever I send a letter to a prospect, I always follow up with a phone call. That alone triples my response rate. Write first, then call and ask questions like, "How long have you had the property? Would you be interested in selling? Can I help out?"

Join Real Estate Associations

Most major cities have a real estate association and/or a landlord association. Who attends the meetings? Investors, landlords, and people who find good deals. Associations are great sources of education, too. At www.shemin.com, we provide a list of real estate associations. Network at their meetings and you will find everything you need to become a successful real estate investor.

CHAPTER 5

A prudent question is one-half of wisdom.
—FRANCIS BACON

Now That You Found It, Analyze It

Do you analyze a property for buying, for selling, or for renting?

The answer is yes . . . for any property. You need to make an analysis with any sale. More important, you need to build in a margin for error. Determine how much money is coming in and going out, but do not buy strictly based on cash flow. You still need to buy a property for less than what it is worth today, so you have room to sell it when you want to.

In addition to margin of error, be aware of the property's finance-ability. The bigger the deals you chase, the more difficult it may be at certain times to get financing. You might have to put what I call *real* (that is, your own) money into it. In fact, on large commercial or investment deals, lenders may insist you put in some of your own cash.

Analysis Paralysis

One of the biggest stumbling blocks of successful investing (and this applies to me, too) is called *paralysis of analysis.* You stumble into a good deal and then you stop dead in your tracks. You think about purchasing, worry about the decision, and *never do* anything.

In my first six months of real estate investing, I looked at hundreds of great deals and I did nothing. How did I know it was a good deal? How did I know I could make money? I was scared to death to make an offer because if I did, I might have actually gotten the deal. Then what?

As we learned earlier, a great deal in real estate is something you can really make money on. There are two approaches to making money in real estate: (1) speculation and (2) investing.

With real estate *speculation,* you buy property that is priced near market value, or put it under contract. For example, you buy something worth half a million dollars for $499,000 and pray that it quickly goes up in value to $550,000 or $600,000.

With real estate *investing,* you look for something you can either put under contract or buy for 20 to 40 percent lower than what it is really worth. That means a property worth $500,000 today would be put under contract for $400,000 or less to make it worthwhile. Face it, if you had to sell this property for $475,000, you would still come out okay because you had a 20 percent margin of error in this deal.

To protect your income source and overcome any analysis paralysis, (1) make sure you have a good deal (because even if it is not as good as you think, you still have a margin of error to work

At Least 20 Percent below Market Value

Rule of thumb: Do not buy property that is not at least 20 or 25 percent below what you really think it is worth today in its current condition. I am not talking about a property worth $100,000 that needs $20,000 worth of work and sells for $80,000. I am talking about having it at least 20 to 25 percent below what it is really worth in today's market.

If you look at enough deals, you will find some well below the value of comparable properties. If you never look and analyze deals, you will not find any.

with), and (2) get lots of information. If I said, "Let me tell you the exact cards that will come out on the blackjack table: Without a doubt, your next hand will be a 19 and the dealer will have 18. The next one, you are going to have 21 and the dealer 18," you would be inclined to play because you would have information about what will happen. This can also happen in real estate investing when you gather lots of meaningful information.

Analyze in Less than 90 Minutes

To analyze any property deal in less than 90 minutes and not get bogged down in analysis paralysis, find the answers to these three questions:

1. What is the property worth today?
2. What repairs are needed, and how much will they cost? (Most properties, even brand-new homes, need repairs.)
3. What can you get it for?

What Is the Property Worth Today?

Remember, to develop a successful real estate investing career, your job is to find deals and put them together. Your job is *not* to become an appraiser, a closing attorney, a management expert, or a repairperson. Use professionals!

Say we parachute you into Naples, Florida. You have never been there before and your goal is to find good deals. What would you do? As discussed in Chapter 4, you look at newspaper ads, drive for dollars, call For Rent ads, For Sale ads, and so on. You are certain to find prospects that may become suspects, so you call one of the property owners, who says, "I think the building is worth $100,000. I will let you have it for $50,000 and it needs very few repairs." But you do not know if it is really worth $100,000. So you call a Realtor who sells a lot of property in that area and ask, "A three-bedroom, two-bath on Apple Street in Naples, Florida— what would it sell for?" He replies, "I've sold two in the last month, one for $99,000 the other for $102,500." You just learned that house is worth about $100,000.

Still, it is important to call two or three people to verify the information you get. Another Realtor might say, "Nothing has sold there in a year. The last offer we got was for $79,900."

If you are looking for commercial property, call a commercial broker or an appraiser and ask, "What would something similar to this property bring in today's market?" Follow up by getting a list of comparable sales in that area from real estate professionals.

How do Realtors, appraisers, and banks determine what a property is worth? They look at comparable sales, usually three to five sales of very similar property close by. Realize that you cannot compare three bedrooms with eight bedrooms; you cannot compare 2-story office buildings with 30-story office buildings. The properties have to be similar.

Take it a step further and get a list of comparable sales. You can actually find lists on the Internet (www.shemin.com) and see the sales price of every property bought or sold (and when it sold) for the street you want information about. In addition, talk with active professionals and ask, "What is the market like?" Then get the information in writing via fax, e-mail, or letter. Put comparable sales lists and information in a folder for future reference.

(Remember, you cannot keep hounding Realtors and never do business with them, so get them to help you and let them have part of the commission.)

After you have done this 15 times in Naples, Florida, you will know the comparables by heart and have rapport with several Realtors.

What Repairs Does It Need?

If you have motivated sellers but their properties need repair, you can find the cost of the repairs from two different sources: from the owner or the seller (most are truthful; a few are not) and from a good contractor who is licensed, bonded, and referred to you. The most important word I just used is *referred*. Make sure you get bids from more than one contractor who comes recommended by respected Realtors or other investors. (Again, you cannot just get bids all the time from contractors and never work with them. Likely you will close on some deals, get repairs done, and give the contractor glowing references. If that does not happen in a timely way, pay the contractors for their written bids.)

What Can You Get It For?

When sellers are motivated to move a property worth $100,000 and it does not need any repairs, they may say, "We'll let you have it for $70,000." (Thirty percent below market value.) Would that be a good deal? Yes. So negotiate an even better deal and get a signed contract. That is where you make your money in real estate.

Before you had access to this book, you may have gotten excited and said, "Oh my God, it's worth $100,000 and it's being offered to me for $70,000! I'm going to sign the contract right now." You would have made some money on this deal, but you would have also made a grave error. By not negotiating, you may have potentially left a lot of money on the table.

Every property's value is in the eyes of its beholder. If you own a lot of real estate and you are being sued, you might make a case that your property is not worth much and needs repairs. On the other hand, if you go to the bank to borrow as much money as you can against the property, you will want it appraised as high as possible using the highest comparable sales. And when the tax assessor calls to figure out your new taxes for next year, you will say the rents are low, the buildings need work, and so on. Since property has different value depending on who is looking at it, make sure you talk to professionals active in the market who tell you honestly what buyers are paying for their properties today.

The best way to determine market value is by attracting an offer through a newspaper ad that includes details of the property. See if the phone rings. Likewise, if you want to see how much rent should be, run a For Rent ad and see if anybody calls. If no one calls, you may not have much of a market.

Put It under Contract

You have negotiated a good price and **put it under contract** with the contingency clause. Now **do your analysis.** Beginners have a tendency to analyze for six weeks before putting in an offer. But by the time they find out the age of the hot water heater and the condition of the roof shingles, and have talked to the neighbors five times, their opportunity may have disappeared.

Instead, at the beginning, do a quick survey to see if it is a good deal, document everything, put your offer in with a contingency, and then do your analysis or due diligence. Remember, if you wait too long, you will lose a lot of deals.

Get Appraisals

Remember, you can always spend a few hundred dollars and get an appraisal done on a property. You may even get the seller to pay for all or part of it. Have a professional appraiser look at it, research comparable sales, and tell you its value. Sometimes when I go to a lender to finance a property, I have the appraisal in hand and can say, "Here's proof. It's worth $200,000. Can I borrow some money, please?"

The Three-Day Deal

When I was asked to be a guest on *The Leeza Gibbons Show* (a TV talk show), Leeza Gibbons challenged me to find a good real estate deal in Los Angeles, California. The producers knew I was from Tennessee and did not know the L.A. real estate market. They also knew I liked to give away homes to homeless people, so they said, "Come out to Los Angeles. If you find a good deal, then you can give a house to a homeless family right on our show." They only gave me three days to put a good deal together.

On my first day, I decided to follow my own advice and drive for dollars in a particular area. I was driving around at six in the morning. When people wearing bathrobes came out of their houses to get their newspapers, I asked them, "What do these houses sell for? I'm looking for a place in this neighborhood." I quickly learned that the worst, cheapest houses in the worst neighborhood started at about $120,000. A little different from Tennessee values. Next, I chased down some For Sale signs and made some calls. After two days, I found three bank foreclosures, one landlord, and four great deals. The best one was a two-bedroom condominium with a pool and tennis court. It appraised for well over $140,000, and I put it under contract for $42,000 with terms from the bank.

How did I determine what real estate values were in that neighborhood? I asked everybody I met, including Realtors, "What are these houses selling for?"

I also needed information about repairs, so a contractor (referred, of course) gave me a written bid for $3,500 to get this condo in tip-top shape.

Third, I negotiated. The bank that was foreclosing on the condo wanted $42,000 to satisfy the loan. I was able to take it over on a short sale because of my good credit. Now this bank can show this as a good loan on their books instead of a bad one.

Then I called back the producers of *Leeza*. At first, they refused to believe me, declaring that "Nothing in Los Angeles sells for under $100,000. You must be making up stories." I had to show them all the paperwork and they finally believed me. We gave that condo to a homeless family, right on the show.

Short Selling

When a bank takes back a property because a loan went bad, often it discounts the property for the amount of the loan. This is referred to as a *short sale* or *short selling*.

Inspect the Property

You want an inspector who is experienced and familiar with repairs to do an inspection of the property. I generally use a licensed, referred, bonded contractor who can make sure the property meets codes and can identify major problems. Also, before closing on any property, I have it inspected for termites.

Get a Clear Title

Make sure you ask the seller, "Do you have clear title to this property?" Sometimes, when you deal with highly motivated sellers, you find out they do not have titles to the properties. They are handling a deal for their uncle, brother, sister, and so on. Either that or they have 22 liens against the property they forgot to tell you about.

Be sure to ask these questions:

- Do you have clear title?
- Are there any loans, liens, or judgments against the property?
- Is there more than one mortgage?

Again, verify everything in writing. And before closing, have an escrow agent do a title search and provide title insurance.

Crunch the Numbers

Real estate investing is real estate by the numbers. You want to know what the profit and loss on a property would be if someone were to buy it, fix it up, and sell it, or if someone should buy it and rent it. Answer all tax, insurance, rental rate, and expense questions. Document all the details so you are an informed buyer. Do this for any property, whether you are going to keep it, wholesale it, lease-option it, or finance it. You want to make sure it will provide cash flow for somebody, even if that somebody is not you.

Gather full details about the transaction costs for buying and selling the property: commission costs (if you work with a Realtor), recording fees (to record deeds), and all financial details that apply to the property, including the terms of any loan (total amount, balance owed, years to pay, interest rate, and so on).

Analysis Recap

When you talk to sellers, always, always, *always ask questions.* The most important questions are: Why are you selling? Why are you selling? Why are you selling? That will determine their motivation level. If sellers say, "I can take my time because I don't really need to sell," they are not motivated. But if they say, "We're moving out of state. Job transfer. Have to sell it in the next three weeks," or "We're going through a divorce," or "We're getting foreclosed on. We've got financial problems," they are most likely motivated.

Then ask, "What is the debt on the property?" If they owe $100,000, it is unlikely they will accept less than $100,000 (or whatever the debt is).

You want to ask, "What are the terms of the loan? What are the payments and interest rate? Are you current on the payments?" Almost every loan has a due-on-sale clause.

The next question is, "Do you have clear title? Whose name is the title in?"

Also ask, "What are the mortgages? Are there additional mortgages, judgments, or liens? What repairs are needed?"

Real Estate Doctor

What if you ask, "What is your mortgage? How much do you owe on the property?" and the seller says, "I'm not going to tell you. This is personal information."

Respond by saying, "I am a real estate doctor and want to help solve a problem. To be able to help you, like a doctor, I have to know your symptoms."

Always enter into the conversation with that intention. If you meet with resistance, say, "By the way, even if you don't want to tell me this information, it's all public information. It's on the Internet. It's at the Registrar of Deeds. I can call the courthouse, the tax assessor's office, and get it anyway. So please go ahead and help me help you. I'm a real estate doctor."

Concerning repairs, make a worksheet and write down the condition of:

- The roof
- The gutters
- The shingles
- The attic
- The ceiling
- The walls
- The electrical system
- The carpet
- The flooring
- The kitchen
- The windows
- The plumbing
- The basement
- The foundation
- The yard

Visualize the house from top to bottom. Ask what work needs to be done and how much it will cost. Then, if you are interested, put it under contract with a contingency and send over your contractor to verify in writing what was found. Get a detailed written bid from your contractor.

All of these items you look for are important to you if you have to finance the property, or sell it, or bring in a partner. Keep all of the details (comparable sales and the repair estimates) in your folder.

Good for Business

By the way, this process reflects how most large commercial deals are handled with big companies involved. They use accountants, lawyers, and other professionals to make sure the numbers are accurate, then close on the deal. That is how you should manage your real estate business.

Most investors want to know everything up front before they put an offer in, but in reality, they do not have to. If you smell a good deal, put your offer in, and conduct your due diligence. However, make sure you have a good deal in hand, because if you put in a lot of offers and never close on them, no one will want to sign another one with you.

CHAPTER 6

It is not for us to forecast the future, but to shape it.
—ANTOINE DE SAINT-EXUPÉRY

How to Control Your Real Estate Holdings

You found it. You analyzed it. Now you want to control it.

Let me give you a secret of real estate investing: You have nothing until you have a signed offer. So many investors, beginners or pros, come to me and say, "I've got a great deal worth $1 million, but I can get it for $200,000. I'm going to make $800,000. I'm going to buy it, rent it out, and make so much money every month. It's going to be great!"

Then I ask: "Do you have it under contract? Do you own it?" They say, "No, I'm going to sign the contract next week." They have nothing—and you will have nothing but a lot of talk and a lot of excitement until you get a signed contract.

The first step in making money in real estate and developing sources of income is controlling the real estate.

Note, I did not say buying it; I did not say signing the deed; I did not say owning it; I did not say borrowing a bunch of money. I said controlling it. When you are in control of something, is that a good thing? Yes. When you own something, is that a good thing? Not necessarily. If you own it, you could be sued, and you are liable for the taxes, the mortgage, and so on. Owning things has its advantages, but simply controlling them is almost always better.

Get a Signed Contract

To get a signed contract, the first step is negotiating one. You will make more money than you have ever made in your life if you follow these simple negotiating strategies.

Negotiating Strategies

When I began in real estate, I found a house worth $80,000 and the owner said, "I'll sell it for $60,000." I thought it was a great deal (it would provide cash flow). I was so excited, I signed the contract immediately. I left a ton of money on the table, though, because I did not know I could negotiate. However, over the years, I learned these basic negotiating rules:

1. The first person who mentions a number loses.
2. Never mention a number until you *absolutely have to.*
3. Ask this magical question as many times as you can until they get upset: "Can you do any better?"
4. You cannot negotiate a good deal until you find out what the seller really needs—what his or her level of pain is.

   People do things for two reasons: One is to get pleasure, and the second is to avoid pain.

They usually sell their property below market value to avoid more pain than they have now. "We have to move. We owe money. We need cash. We're getting divorced."

When you negotiate with sellers, you want to be like a doctor and find out about their symptoms and situation. Be sure to ask: "Why are you selling? How long do you have to sell? When do you need to sell the property by? What are you going to do after you sell? What will you do with the money? How long have you been trying to sell the property? Have you received any offers?"

When you are discussing these points, keep asking questions but say very little. "When did you buy the property? What did you pay for it?" If the other person does not want to give you that information, say it is all public record anyway, and besides, you intend to improve their situation.

Ask: "What is the mortgage on the property?" Knowing that helps you figure out the lowest price the sellers are likely to accept. If the mortgage owed is $80,000, they probably will not sell it for less than $80,000. Likewise, if they bought it for $20,000 five years ago, they are probably not going to sell for under $20,000.

Negotiating Price

Ask the next question this way: "What is the absolute least amount you would take for this property?" Then pause. Let the silence eat up the moment and eat at the sellers. People do not like silence; it makes them nervous. So just wait until they come up with something. It could be 10 seconds, or it could be two minutes. However, they *will* answer.

What do you do next? You pause, look at them, grunt a little, sigh, act uncomfortable, and say, "Uh, can you do any better?" Remain silent and look at them. What if they say, "No, $68,000 is the least we can do. That's it. That's the least we'll take," then what do you do? Sigh again and ask, "Really? What is the *absolute least* amount you would?" They might say, "OK, we'll tell you what . . . $67,000. That's it." How long did it take you to make that extra thousand dollars? Between 5 and 15 seconds. Not a bad return for your time.

Okay, they said $67,000. What do you do now? Start over and ask the question again: "Can you do any better?" Suppose they get upset, even angry, because you have asked the same question seven times. Simply smile, laugh, and say, "Just kidding."

So when sellers are irritated and say they are at their absolute bottom number, you know you have hit their lowest price. But you are not finished. You counter with a number that is a lot lower than their final price. And always use unusual numbers.

Why do I use odd numbers? Because people think I know something they do not know, that I have a secret formula. So if their lowest price is $67,000 and they insist, "That's it," I come back and say, "Great. I'll offer $57,426."

You may be chuckling and thinking this is cute, but negotiating will prove to be the most money you ever make in your life—per second, per minute, per hour, per week, per year. Because when I say my number, they ask, "How did you come up with that?" I reply, "I just have my secret formula." They might say, "I can't do $57,426 (or whatever that weird number is), but I can do $63,000. Take it or leave it." I come back again with a still lower number and gamble

Reframe the Situation

If your children have ever become mad at you because you told them 20 times to brush their teeth, it is unlikely they would show their frustration by laughing. However, if you say (in a playful way), "If you don't brush your teeth, I'm going to spank you, put you in boarding school, then send you to your grandparents for five hundred years . . ." what will they do? They will laugh. I call this *reframing*. This technique works well in negotiations because it lowers the tension, lightens the conversation, and makes people feel better.

that I will save another couple of thousand dollars. If they stick to their last number five more times, then I quit negotiating.

You want to **negotiate, negotiate, negotiate,** and if you do not like to negotiate verbally, do it in writing. Send your offers by mail or e-mail instead. Mail a hundred offers a week. If someone wants $100,000, write an offer for $49,872 with a contingency clause (which I will explain) in it. If you get a signed offer, you have made a great deal. This is an excellent way to gain a lot of real estate.

Standard Buyer's Contract

Make your contract a form of income for you. If you are buying a property, write at the top of the contract "Standard Buyer's Contract" and follow these directions.

Buying Property: Seller Pays Closing Costs

In your buyer's contract, the seller pays for everything, including title insurance and all closing costs. Usually, closing and title insurance costs are split between the buyer and seller, but that does not have to be the case. If it is a rental property, the seller gives the buyer all of the tenants' deposits and the entire month's rent for whenever it is going to close (e.g., if you close on the 15th of January, the contract says you get all of January's rents).

I promise you, if you do not include these requirements in your contract, you will never get them. Even if you *do* include them, you will still only get them some of the time. Negotiating these costs can save you hundreds of dollars on every transaction.

Make Offers via E-Mail

I have a student who sends out 100 offers a week via e-mail. About 90 percent of them go unanswered and 5 percent are answered by recipients (usually Realtors) calling to cuss him out. But 1 or 2 percent make counteroffers, and people often accept ridiculously low prices. Could you do that, too?

Often people sign a contract without really reading it. In the early years of my real estate dealings, someone gave me a standard contract and I went to closing without reading it. Guess who paid for everything? I did. I certainly learned the hard way. I recommend you use your standard contract, and you may not even have to negotiate all of the details.

Earnest Money

Do you have to put earnest money in a contract? No. The contract is valid without earnest money. However, a lot of Realtors will insist, "I need to make sure you're serious. Put some earnest money down." Again, in most cases, you have a choice—use your own money, or use OPM.

I just put a house valued at $600,000 under contract. The Realtor wanted a lot of earnest money, so I asked him, "How much interest will you pay me on that money?" He said, "I won't pay any interest." So I replied, "I earn about 36 to 40 percent on my money through different real estate investments. That is about 3 percent a month." Would a Realtor be willing to pay that much? Not likely.

Selling Property: Buyer Pays Closing Costs

If you are selling property, you still use your standard contract, but this time, you say the buyer pays the title insurance and closing costs. If it is rental property, the *buyer* gets the deposits but *you collect the rent* for the full month. Type in what you want. You may not get everything you ask for, but if you never ask, you will never get it.

Negotiating Owner's Terms

Now that you have negotiated on price, it is time to negotiate on terms. Whenever you are doing a contract, ask for "owner's terms." Even if you are going to pay cash, even if you are going to wholesale it to someone else, always get owner's terms. That means the *seller*

Only Negotiate with the Decision Maker

Always make sure you are dealing with the person who has the legal authority to sell the property. If anyone else is involved, make sure you negotiate with that person, too. You will save a lot of time and hassle when you communicate directly with decision makers.

Try this: Go to a car dealership, a stereo place, a restaurant, or a major department store and approach the manager. Ask how much one of the items costs and say, "What's the least you'll take?" "It's listed for $50, so I want $50." Respond by saying, "Can you do any better?" Sometimes the manager will hold firm, but sometimes you might hear this: "Well, we *are* going to run a sale in three weeks and list it for $29.99, so give me $30 today and it's yours."

If you do not negotiate, you will not ever get the lower price that you want. If you negotiate on a real estate deal, you could save thousands of dollars.

lends you the money to buy the property. You put the least possible amount of money down, so instead of coming up with $100,000 to buy a property, you might put $5,000 down and pay $700 a month.

Most often when you negotiate on owner's terms, the sellers need cash. So you ask this million-dollar question: "What will you do with the cash?" Here is one answer I have heard: "I need $4,000 to pay off a Visa bill, and then the rest I'm not sure about." I have learned what that person needs; he just told me about the "pain" he is dealing with. So I say, "I'll give you $4,000 down so you can pay off your Visa bill, then I'll pay you $600 a month for the term of the loan." That met his needs and I did not require much cash as a down payment.

When sellers say, "We're going to invest the cash in a CD and make 5 percent," I ask, "How would you like to earn 7 or 8 percent?" They reply by saying, "That sounds great. How are you going to do that?" I respond, "Through owner's terms. Your loan is secured by your real estate, which you are familiar with, and I will pay you 7½ percent, better than the bank." By structuring a deal this way through owner's terms, I help them meet their needs.

Contingency Clauses

On the subject of contracts, let's talk about how to reduce your risk to zero, because I know you are thinking, "Wait a minute. I'm not sure. What if I make a bad offer? What if it isn't a good deal? What if it doesn't rent? What if I am going to lose money?"

Would you be interested in a business if your risk was reduced to zero? The way you do that in real estate is by writing your contract with a *contingency clause*. This clause is also called a *weasel clause*. I rarely sign a contract without one.

In the contract, the contingency clause may say something like this:

- "This contract is contingent upon buyer's inspection and approval before closing . . ."
- "This contract is contingent upon buyer's partner's inspection and approval before closing . . ."
- "This contract is contingent upon buyer receiving favorable financing . . ."

Their messages are all the same: "This is not what I thought it was. It does not work for me. I am out of here." With this clause, you are not obligated to close on a deal if it does not work for you.

Financing Contingencies

Many contracts include a financing contingency: If you do not get proper financing, you do not close on the home. Be careful how often you do this, though. Do not ruin your reputation by putting in offers on properties that you know you cannot close on.

Most people, after signing a contract, choose to close 30 days later. I recommend you type 90 days instead of 30 days into your buyer's contract. Why? Often people who say they will be able to close in 30 days do not do so. In fact, half of all real estate contracts fail because buyers do not get their financing in time.

A Realtor's Objection

A Realtor in Miami told one of my students, "Wait a minute. I know you real estate investors like to put in these contingency clauses, but I'm not going to allow it." My student countered, "Listen. What if a hurricane, a flood, a fire, or even vandals come the day before closing, break all of the windows, tear up the property? You mean to say I'd still have to buy it even with these problems? So, just please let me come by the day that we close to check that everything is still OK. I'm a professional real estate investor who's going to close on it if everything seems right, don't worry about that." Yes, it is fair to put in that contingency clause, no matter what a Realtor says.

With a good deal and giving yourself 90 days to close, you can find something to do with that property, like lining up a buyer. You risk not closing, but since you have control of the property, you have reduced *your* risk to zero.

Contract for Deed

When you are buying a property, your first preference is always to get the deed to the property. If the seller will not give you the deed (possibly because the mortgage has due-on-sale clauses), then turn to a lease option (discussed in the following section).

Here is an example of a contract for deed, sometimes called a *land contract*.

Mr. Smith owns the house he bought 10 years ago for $50,000. It is worth $100,000 today. You say, "Mr. Smith, I'll buy it from you for $70,000," and he agrees. But instead of borrowing the money, you give Mr. Smith a contract that says, "I will pay you $700 a month for x number of years until I pay all $70,000. I will have the house under contract for deed."

So who owns the house? You do. You get all the benefits of ownership, and, after you fulfill the terms of the contract, you get the deed. This is a type of owner's terms. (Remember, *owner's terms* refers to the seller lending you the money to buy the property.)

Controlling Properties with Options

Most commercial and industrial property is not controlled with contracts, but with options. An option gives you the *right* to buy something but *not the obligation.* So if you see a $40 million office building and put an option in to buy it at $30 million within one year, the seller will sign and you have one year to buy it for $30 million. Then, whenever you find someone who will pay you $32 million for it, you exercise your option and give the seller $30 million.

Sometimes sellers want a down payment before allowing you to option a piece of property. However, if you are a good negotiator, you will make the down payment as low as possible.

> *Remember, a contract with a contingency is almost like an option because you are not obligated to buy.*

Control with a Lease

You can control property through a lease. You also could re-lease it for more than what you have leased it for (if your lease gives you the right to sublease). This is another way to make money.

Control with Lease Options

You could lease a property for $500 a month for five years with the option to buy it. You could also have the right to sublease it for $800 or $1,000 a month or so.

If you lease a property for five years with the option to buy it, you *do not own* it. What if the world goes into a massive depression? Suppose you bought the property with borrowed money and then were obligated to pay it back? You would be in hot water because you would own the property and would have an obligation to pay. With a lease option, even if a depression hits and the property value

Getting Out of a Lease

Do people get out of leases? Yes. However, I am not recommending you do a lease option just so you can walk away from it. I recommend doing it because you have the freedom of not being tied to the property like the owner would be. You have less liability and risk. And if you have done your homework and have lease-optioned it properly, you will make money. So it is possible to get out of a lease, but it is not usually smart.

goes down by half, you still have an option to buy but no obligation. (Read Chapter 8 for more in-depth discussion of lease options.)

Disclose Everything in Writing

My general rule for everything you do is this: Disclose everything in writing.

For example, if I lease-option property from Bill, I have a five-year lease with a five-year option to buy it, then I turn to Susie and say, "Susie, would you like to become a homeowner? You can lease-option or buy the property from me. Give me $5,000 down and $1,000 a month." She is now a homeowner who has owner's terms or some kind of ownership in the property. What if Bill (whom I got the property from) suddenly goes bankrupt, gets divorced, or has the IRS chasing him, and he cannot pass clear title? At the same time, Susie says, "I'm ready to exercise my option. I want to buy the property." I would have to say, "I can't sell you the property because I don't have title to it, Bill does, and he is having some financial difficulties." Susie is upset and says, "Hey, I thought you were going to sell me the house." Through these actions, I have committed fraud. That is why you always disclose everything in writing any time you exchange information with someone: a mortgage banker, a title lawyer, a buyer, or a seller. If you do not, you will regret it.

Proper Title Disclosure

Always make sure there is proper title disclosure for any transaction. Some real estate investors are going to prison for fraud because they did not properly disclose title information. Learn the proper way to do this and you will stay out of trouble.

In my standard buyer's contracts, I write this on the top of the cover page:

(1) "I am a real estate investor. I am buying your property and I may resell it or rerent it for a profit. You understand that."

(2) "I do not represent you or your interests."

Have I disclosed everything I am doing?

When I am going to sell a property (using a standard seller's contract) or lease-option it, I also state in writing:

(1) "I am a real estate investor who invests in real estate to make money."

(2) "I do not represent you or your interests."

(3) "I may or may not have or be able to obtain good title to this property."

Most people say I am being overly cautious, but I strongly believe in disclosing everything in writing.

Three Review Points

1. Negotiate a contract. Negotiate, negotiate, negotiate. You can always get a lower price. If the seller quickly accepts your price, you have not negotiated enough.

2. Always try to get owner's terms.

3. Always include contingency clauses to reduce your risk.

Disclosures Rarely Stop a Deal

You might say, "Wait a minute. If you put these disclosures in your contracts, no one will sign them." Not in the real world! Most people are motivated for their own reasons. If a buyer wants to become a homeowner, he or she is willing to overlook that clause. Motivated sellers want their money. You have found their pain. They are willing to go ahead. But if you do not disclose everything and something bad happens, you could be in big trouble. It's called fraud.

If you cannot do these things, then you have to make a business decision based on all your information and decide if it is worth it for you to proceed or walk away. Rule of thumb: **Always have more pending deals than you can do.**

Also, be sure to understand how to control properties by contracts, contract for deed, and putting in contingency clauses, options, and lease options. Make sure you disclose everything. Never, *ever* close on a property without getting the proper title insurance and having the proper insurance in place to protect you.

CHAPTER 7

Big shots are only little shots who keep shooting.
—CHRISTOPHER MORLEY

Multiple Real Estate Profit Centers

Most people think that there are only a few ways to make money, but there are lots of them, especially in real estate. For beginning investors, I recommend wholesaling properties, also referred to as *flipping* or *quick turning*. With this approach, you are not using any of your own money or your own credit to buy property. In effect, you get paid to find good deals and have almost no risk if you disclose everything properly. You can use this approach to get into real estate, learn about real estate, generate cash, and so on. You can also consider other strategies (e.g., buy, fix, and sell; buying and holding; getting involved in financing mortgages).

Quick-Turning or Flipping Strategy

Did you realize almost everything you buy is wholesaled or flipped, including your chairs, your furniture, your televisions, and more? In these cases, a businessperson went to companies in China, Japan, Korea, or even locally and put them under contract to make items, then sold those items to a retail store for a marked-up price.

Similarly, car dealerships put their cars on a lot for sale. They get vehicles from the manufacturer without putting any money down. They have finance plans with the manufacturers for, for instance, $20,000 per car, then they sell that car to a buyer for $25,000. That's called *wholesaling, quick turning,* or *flipping.* Most industries are doing business this way, including real estate.

Here's an example. Suppose John finds a property worth $100,000. It needs $20,000 worth of repairs, and John has it under contract for $40,000; therefore, he plans to put $60,000 into it and sell it for $100,000.

John has a few choices. He can borrow the money, rely on his credit, or use his cash to buy the property. He also has to hire a contractor to do repairs (or do the work himself) for an estimated $20,000. However, he goes into cost overruns, the repairs end up being $25,000 and take six months to complete. He has put $65,000 into the property, but it's still a great deal. He then puts this fixed-up house on the market, sells it for $100,000 three months later, and makes about $35,000. However, he's had carrying costs, holding costs, taxes, insurance, and other headaches. He has spent nine months worrying about the property and dealing with contractors, Realtors, and prospective buyers. He also has had to pay some commissions, so he really only has made about $27,000. Is that still a good deal for John? Absolutely. However, he has spent nine months to get his capital investment back and earn his profit.

Time is money. Your single asset in business is your time. What's your time worth? After having access to unlimited riches in real estate, John has learned that instead of buying, fixing, and selling properties, he can wholesale them. Let's consider an alternate scenario: John puts the property under contract for $40,000. He gets bids and estimates repairs. He also does sales comparatives. Then he runs an ad in the paper that says, "Handyman special. Won't last. Call now." His phone rings off the hook with investors who love to buy and fix up property. John asks them, "This house is worth well over $100,000. What would you pay for it as is?" One may offer $45,000, another $49,000, yet another $52,000. He next asks the investor willing to pay $52,000, "What are you going to do with it?" The investor replies, "Assuming I can do the repairs for $20,000, I'll have $72,000 into it. Then I think I can sell it for $105,000 because real estate values in that neighborhood are going up."

After starting negotiations with this prospective buyer, John asks, "What's the absolute most you would pay for this? Can you do any better? Can you do any better? Can you do any better?" The investor replies, "Instead of $52,000, I can afford to pay $54,000." John returns with, "I was really hoping to get $62,849." The prospective buyer says, "This is my last offer. I'll pay $55,000 and spend $20,000 fixing it. I'll have $75,000 in it, sell it for $105,000, and make between $20,000 and $25,000."

John writes out the standard seller's contract stating a price of $55,000. The buyer agrees to pay the closing costs, and John gives him 10 days to close. An attorney arranges the closing, called a *collapsed closing*. The buyer comes in with $55,000, and the attorney hands $40,000 over to the original sellers of the property. Are they happy? Yes, they got what they wanted. John gets $15,000 because he put together a good deal that had a lot of margin to work with. He disclosed everything in writing, told all parties what he was doing, did some negotiating, and made $15,000.

This transaction took about 30 days. John spent nothing out of his pocket and had no risk. He didn't have to fight with contractors, drive by the property, make sure everything was fixed right, or deal with selling it. Instead of making $25,000 or $27,000 over nine months, he made $15,000 over one month. Better yet, his stress level was a lot less than the first scenario because he was wholesaling, not financing and renovating. John basically got paid for finding a good deal.

Get Contracts with No Money Down

When I started in real estate in the early 1990s, a gentleman named Larry, about the same age as I (27 or 28 at the time), visited owners of office buildings around downtown Nashville, Tennessee, and asked, "What would you sell your building for?" If they said, "Two million dollars," he'd reply, "What's the least you'd take for the office building? Can you do any better?" They'd say $1.8 million and he'd get an option to buy that building for $1.8 million for six months without putting any money down.

Then Larry would run an ad in a German newspaper inviting Germans to invest in American real estate in Nashville. This ad generated calls from several overseas investors. To follow up, he would send them a photo of the building with all the details spelled out, including rents and answers to questions that an investor would ask about the property. He also included some comparable sales on the flyer. Then he would ask, "What would you pay for a building like this?" They might respond with $2.4 million or $2.2 million, or whatever. Larry would then get a contract and work with a good commercial closing attorney. After he closed the deal, he would make anywhere from $200,000 to $800,000 on each building. In just a few years, he flipped or wholesaled about seven of them and made a lot of money. However, he had a lawsuit served against him because a German investor said, "We thought you were representing us. We did not know you were wholesaling and making money."

What is the lesson here? You must write into all of your contracts a statement such as "I do not represent you or your interests." If Larry had included that statement in his contracts, he wouldn't have been sued, or he would have won the lawsuit.

Turning Properties That You Control but Don't Own

These four steps are required to quick-turn, flip, or wholesale a property. Some aspects have been discussed in earlier chapters.

1. Find a good deal.
2. Get it under contract.
3. Find buyers for it.
4. Close the sale.

Can you close on a property that you do not own? Yes, because though you do not own it, you *control* it because you have it under contract, as in John's situation. You can accomplish this either through an attorney or an escrow agent who helps you assign/sell the contract to the next person or use a collapsed closing.

In general, all contracts are assignable in the United States. So for the first option, you can say, "I have a contract to buy this house for $40,000. Give me $15,000 and I'll give you the right to buy the house for $40,000." These days, many commercial properties are sold and purchased by assigning the option or the contract. You are simply selling your contract.

The second option, a collapsed closing, requires two closings, two contracts, and two deeds. The end buyer walks into the closing meeting and pays the money for the property. The original seller is paid by the wholesaler (that's John in the preceding example), then John sells it simultaneously to the end buyer at the same meeting. Two closings happen within 30 minutes, and funds go from the buyer to John to the original seller.

Many mortgage companies do not like flips or wholesale deals, so you might structure the transaction in a way that requires the end buyer to purchase the property for $55,000. That way, there is only one contract on the closing statement and John gets a

$15,000 finder's fee. With this scenario, the property has only been sold once.

Start Marketing

When you have a property under contract, start marketing it immediately. Create a flyer about the property, including a photo and description. Say something like, "Will appraise at $100,000, maybe $110,000. Must sell. Make an offer. Only needs $8,000 of repairs. Will rent for $900 a month."

You can even take photos with a digital camera and put them and your flyer on the Internet. If you cannot do this, have a Realtor do it. Answer all possible questions on that flyer, then fax, mail, or e-mail it. Call all of your potential buyers, especially Realtors and people you met at association meetings. Set a convenient time and say, "I'll be at the property Saturday, 12:00 to 12:15." If 10 investors show up at 12:00, that is good.

One investor who buys properties can purchase all or most of the deals that you find. You only need good deals. Serious investors will buy a lot of those deals, so you don't need to know a large number of them.

Make Preapprovals Mandatory

A word of caution: Never sign a contract to sell anything to anyone unless that person has been preapproved from a bank or a mortgage company for financing the property. Alternatively, you need proof that the purchaser has cash to pay for the property. Ask this question: "Oh, you're going to pay cash? I want written proof, a bank statement, or whatever, of where the cash is coming from. Don't sign the contract until you have that proof. Mail, fax, or deliver it to my office." I guarantee that you will save yourself from headaches if you do that. Also, make sure that you verify in writing what people tell you.

Cure for the Doubting Spouse

Suppose your spouse, loved one, or significant other is scared about your getting into real estate. He or she thinks it's risky and fights you every step of the way. How do you deal with the doubting spouse and/or any other dissenting family members? Don't tell them in detail everything you're going to do; just do it. Then, when you flip your first property, tell them about it and give them the check.

My student Bob has a lovely wife Cindy, who once said, "That flipping stuff's got to be illegal. It's got to be wrong. There's no way you can do it. Don't get involved. I don't want you doing it."

Still, Bob went out and flipped his first property. He found a house worth about $80,000, paid $65,000, flipped it, wholesaled it, and made about $7,000. Then he went to Cindy and said, "I wholesaled a house and closed on it." She said, "I told you not to do that. You can't do it. It's wrong. There's no money in it. I'm sure that stuff doesn't work." Bob replied, "Cindy, I'd like to give you the check for $7,000 that I made. You take it. You spend it any way you want to."

Now, every morning Cindy wakes up and says, "Bob, how many houses are you going to flip today? Why did you only make $5,000 on that one? You gave away too much. You could have flipped it and made $8,000. Get out there and find some more deals."

Bob and Cindy's example suggests how you can respond to dissenting or negative family members: Give them the check. All of a sudden, they'll become more interested in real estate investing. Cindy did . . . and she is still married to Bob.

Buy-Fix-and-Sell Strategy

Think like a real estate wholesaler getting properties ready for retail sale. Find houses that need painting, cleaning, and fixing, then sell them at retail price. On a single-family home, for example, you should make an average of $12,000 to $25,000 for a house that would sell in the $50,000 to $100,000 range. If you have a house in the $100,000 to $150,000 range, you should make $20,000 to $30,000 after you buy it, fix it up, and sell it. If it is in the $200,000 to $300,000 range, you should make between $20,000 and $50,000. For commercial buildings that sell between $0.5 million and $2 million, you could make from $30,000 up to as much as $80,000, depending on your capital, your time, and the overhead involved. However, if you can't make a good amount of money on the deal, it may not be worth your time. Make sure you get paid not only for the use of your time, but also for the use of your capital.

Know the Costs

When you buy a house to fix up and sell, you need to know the following costs:

- Carrying costs
- Taxes
- Insurance
- Repairs (give yourself room for cost overruns)
- Transaction costs (closing costs to buy it, closing costs to sell it, commissions)

Calculate at what price you think you can sell the house, how long it will take you to sell it, your cost of capital, and your payment to yourself. If you are spending 20 hours a month working at the house or running back and forth, what's your time worth? $10? $20? $100 an hour? Multiply that number into the equation to decide whether this buy-fix-and-sell property will be profitable for you.

I have met a lot of real estate investors who have told me stories like this one: "I bought a house for $50,000, spent $20,000 fixing it, and sold it for $90,000. I made $20,000. It only took me a year and a half. I worked on it every day, six days a week, did all the painting and carpeting myself." I say "Congratulations. You just bought yourself a $6-an-hour job."

That is not what savvy real estate investors do. Your job is to find good deals, put them together, and sell them. If you want to be a drywaller or a painter, then spend time learning how to do these skills, especially in the beginning. There's nothing wrong with that. In fact, many investors start by doing their own work because they have to hold on to their money. However, remember your goal: Do you want to be a cleaner, painter, and drywaller, or do you want to be an investor who makes money?

> *To summarize, make sure that there's a big enough margin in the deal for your profit, your overhead, your time, and your cost of capital. Also, verify that your contractors' bids are accurate and that you can rely on reputable repair people. Allow extra time and money for this strategy because repairs always take longer than you think.*

Dealing with Contractors

When people buy property to fix up, their biggest complaint is dealing with contractors. That's why I suggest you make sure that every repair bid is in writing, that you have a fixed finish date for each part of the job, and that you never give your contractors more money than the work that has been done. Draw out payment every week as they do the work; never advance them too much. If you do, they won't finish the job because they've already been paid.

In addition, if they don't finish by the date they promised in writing, have a per-day penalty, just as the government has. When city, county, and state governments build new facilities, they use holdbacks and per-day penalties because, for every day your property is unfinished, it is a day you cannot sell or rent it. You're losing money, so you need to deduct a per-day penalty from the money you owe the contractor. Again, have everything in writing, and most important, make sure that you are working with referred, licensed, bonded, and insured contractors.

Use Other People's Money

The best way to buy and hold (or even buy and fix up) property is through other people's money (OPM). You could own 10 houses in your name and be on the hook for 10 loans at $100,000 apiece. Alternatively, you could get a partner who puts up the $1 million. Instead of putting your name on the loan or mortgage and using your credit, use OPM. Have a silent partner with whom you can work. You make all of the decisions, use your energy to fix up and sell the property, pay back your partner's initial investment, and split the profits. Your silent partner holds the property in his/her name, and you receive a written agreement that's filed at the courthouse. For example, the agreement might state you each have a 50 percent interest in the income and equity of the property. When that property sells, you are entitled to half of the profit. When it's rented, you get half of the rent and pay half of the expenses. How much money comes out of your pocket? None.

Be sure to carefully analyze any deal you make, running through all the numbers regarding what comes in and what goes out. That way, both you and your partner have a clear idea on how the money will flow. Warn your partner (as I am warning you) that it is likely that you will spend more money than you think and always make less money than you predict, as in any business—and especially in real estate. However, you will make money if you do it right. Occasionally, a deal will make a lot more money than you thought. It all works out.

Offer an Incentive

To make the partnership attractive, you can give the person who puts up the money the advantages of writing off expenses and depreciation on his or her taxes. You may want to form a legal corporation or partnership so you can give your partner certain income tax benefits, yet you still own half of the property and half of the income.

You might be able to negotiate with your partner for more than 50 percent of the profit and income. Just do what is fair and right. Remember the saying "Pigs get fat, hogs get slaughtered." I believe there is plenty of money for everyone involved, if you are able to find good deals.

Buying-and-Holding Strategy

When you decide to buy and hold property, you have the advantage of building a lot of wealth because every month the debt goes down, the property appreciates, and the cash comes in. Would you like to have several rental properties that generate thousands of dollars a month so you can use that money to pay expenses, pay off debts, and have extra cash flow every month? If you don't want to manage the property, you can hire a management company and manage the manager. You can be free from dealing with tenants and still receive income every month.

Owning property remains one of the best wealth builders available. It can be a great way to build up an education or a retirement fund for children, grandchildren, or favorite relatives. You can even buy a house in their names and, in about 15 years, they will have a paid asset worth a lot more than you paid for it.

Understand, though, that buying and holding property can be a roller-coaster ride. Sometimes properties are vacant; sometimes tenants and repairs create headaches for you. However, over the long term, if they generate enough cash flow and enough equity, they will make you rich.

Financing Mortgages as a Strategy

Every time you buy or sell a property, it is likely that there is some type of mortgage on it. You can profit from these mortgages. For many years, while I was buying or selling properties, I referred between 30 and 80 people a year to a particular mortgage company. After a while, I decided to become a mortgage originator (i.e., someone who finds people needing mortgages). This mostly requires filling out some paperwork. The processor actually processes the mortgages, but the originator gets a fee ranging anywhere from 30 to 70 percent of the mortgage amounts for finding customers. On a $100,000 loan, for example, that fee could be 1 point ($1,000), 2 points ($2,000), or even from 3 to 5 points (from $5,000 to $7,000).

Start by becoming affiliated with a mortgage company that does good work and that hires people who are honest and dependable. By becoming a mortgage originator, every time a mortgage is completed, you earn those fees.

> *Remember, any time you make money at something, be sure to disclose your role to your clients by saying, "I recommend this mortgage company. I'm an originator. I get paid for recommending the loan to you."*

Owner Financing

If you live in the world of real estate, you will find people who either give you or already have owner-financing notes. As an example, you could put $1,000 down on a $100,000 price, and the lender would give you $99,000 on a $100,000 purchase for 30 years at 10 percent interest. You can then broker that loan and earn a fee for doing it. Start by calling on people who buy those mortgages (they advertise in local newspapers, or ask around for referrals), and ask, "What would you pay for this type of loan?" They might reply, "We're going to discount it. We'll pay $94,000." Then you call the property owners and ask, "What's the least amount you would take if we could get that cash in your hands right now?" They reply, "We'll take $90,000." You write up the contracts, then have the mortgage company that is buying the loan arrange the legalities and close it for you. They pay you $94,000, and you pay the property owners $90,000. You will make about $4,000 on that mortgage transaction.

Mortgages as a Source of Income

Mortgages are bought and sold every minute in the United States. In fact, when you first got a loan on your home, the bank or loan company probably sold it immediately. Stop letting them make all the money and get into the action, too.

In addition to being a mortgage originator, I also buy loans. If you have a pending mortgage opportunity, go to www.shemin.com, or call and tell us what you've got. We'll either make a bid on it or find others to buy your loans.

Some people make a living brokering notes like this by running ads and finding owner-held financing. When you're talking to potential investors and sellers, simply ask "By the way, do you have owner-held financing or do you know anyone who has it and would like to sell it?" When they answer yes, ask for details. Write down the basic terms of the note [e.g., type of mortgage (first or second mortgage), characteristics of the property behind it, value of the property, terms (amount, payment, principal, interest, years left on the note, who has signed it), and creditworthiness of the noteholder]. Then ask us for a quote on the note. We'll help you determine what your profit can be.

Seven Secrets for Getting Paid

1. *Residual income.* The beauty of buying and holding property is that it generates residual income. One of the problems with wholesaling or buying, fixing, and selling property is the absence of ongoing or residual income. Therefore, if you turn a property and make a few thousand dollars, you still have no money coming in the next month from that property. Remember residual income creates happiness (RICH)? One of your themes for real estate investing should be RICH.

   How would you like to have the best of both worlds? Let me explain. A few years ago, a student located 20 duplexes in disrepair. The owners were motivated to sell because the buildings were run-down. They were willing to sell them for $20,000 each, owner's terms.

Each unit was actually worth about $40,000 or $50,000, so my student put the property under contract for $20,000 and flipped most of the units to me for about $28,000 each. My student made $160,000 ($8,000 × 20) by quick-turning that deal. I received a good deal because I got property worth more than the price I paid. The original sellers got what they wanted, too. In fact, one of the sellers wrote us a letter thanking us for taking those horrible duplexes off his hands. We then whole-saled these units to another investor and made about $60,000 ($3,000 per duplex × 20). The end buyer of the duplexes fixed them up and raised the rents tremendously. In a matter of three years, the duplexes increased in value to $120,000 each. The end buyer later sold those 20 properties and made more than $1 million, all because of the deal my student found. Some might think I should be upset by that result because I only made $60,000 and the end buyer made $1 million. That did not seem fair. I learned from that experience to develop a strategy of sitting down with prospective property buyers and walking them through the numbers, saying, "Mr. and Mrs. Investor, you're going to buy these duplexes for $60,000, and they'll be worth $100,000 or more in a few years. You'll make a lot of money. Isn't that great? One way I get paid for bring-ing these great opportunities to you is through a fee. It doesn't come out of your pocket until you sell or refinance the prop-erty. My fee would be five percent of the sales price whenever you sell or refinance these properties. That could be in a year or two, or even three years from now.

"We'll put a note against the property and record it at the courthouse. The lawyer will handle all of this. Whenever you refinance or sell the property, I get an extra fee for helping you get this great deal in the first place. Realize that you'll make most or all of the money—about $20,000 per building—and I'll only get, say, $4,000, assuming it sells for $90,000 or so."

This approach is almost like getting a second mortgage recorded against the property with your name, address, and phone number. Because of the recording, the buyers cannot sell that property or refinance it until they pay the fee.

Ask for this kind of deal every time you wholesale or sell a property. Have your attorney draw up the paperwork. You will not always get the purchaser's agreement, but what if you get it a few times? You then get paid again on the property you have already received payment on.

Be sure to disclose everything in writing and check with your own attorney to make sure you can do it. I have done this a few times and enjoyed getting a call or letter stating, "Please sign this paper. We need to pay you your $9,000 because we can't sell the property or refinance it until you release your lien."

What if the sale took place 10 years previously and the property increased in value to $1 million? Five percent of that would be $50,000—not bad. Suppose you request this residual income and the prospective buyer asks, "Why should I let you get paid again when the property sells?" Your reply would be, "How much do you think this will be worth in five years from now? If it's worth $100,000 then and you're buying it for $60,000 now, you're going to make $40,000. So do you really mind paying someone $5,000 to make $40,000? If that isn't a good deal for you, I know a lot of other buyers who'd like to get into this deal."

The buyer might say, "No way. I'm greedy; I'm not going to give you anything. I want to make all of the money." Then you make a choice: Either wholesale the property to that person without taking the residual income, or move on to somebody else. However, I promise you this: If you never *ask* for the residual, you will never get it. If you ask for it every time, you will get it sometimes. That "sometimes" could be worth $2,000, $5,000, $10,000, or even $20,000.

2. *Make three offers.* Whenever you make an offer on a property, don't just make one offer. Make three. For example, if

the sellers want $100,000 for their house, make one offer for $64,500 in cash. Make a second offer with $1,000 down at $65,922. Make a third offer with nothing down and $800 a month for $68,422. You have given them three choices: the cash offer being the lowest, the second one with terms a little higher, and the third one with terms higher still. When you sell a property, do the same thing: Say, "If you give me cash, pay me a wholesale flip fee, and agree to a residual fee, it's this particular price; if you don't give me that, it's another price."

3. *Become a mortgage broker.* Some states require a license, certificates, and educational classes to become a mortgage broker whereas others don't. The same is true to be a mortgage originator. Consult with your attorney or mortgage company, or call the mortgage department at the department of commerce and insurance in your state and find out the requirements.

   Generally, you can affiliate with several mortgage brokers and become an originator without too many regulations. Mainly, you want to affiliate with reputable brokerage companies and get referral fees from them. That's how to develop another source of real estate revenue. You can get referral fees from contractors and title companies, too. Just make sure they are run by honest people who deliver great service.

4. *Put service before money.* More important than making lots of money is delivering quality service to your clients. If you give good service, you *will* make money; if you give bad service, you will be out of business. Remember, always disclose any referral or relationship fee in writing to your clients.

5. *Choose a geographic focus.* As a beginner, should you concentrate on one small area, view the whole city as your territory, or consider the whole state or country as your domain? The answer: Do what you feel comfortable with.

   Initially, I picked a moderate-income neighborhood in Nashville on which to focus. It only took me a few weeks to know the neighborhood and the prices in it. However, I realized the people who make the most money have more guts than beginners, and they make bigger deals. Before long, I expanded beyond the first targeted neighborhood. I now view the whole world as my territory, so when I travel and go on vacation, I often find a deal, then wholesale it or lease-option it.

I suggest that you first concentrate on smaller deals in a certain area before branching out into, for instance, large apartment buildings in exotic locations. However, be careful not to spend all your time chasing elephants—big deals that never happen.

6. *Find the right advisors.*   How do you find title and mortgage brokering companies that will do double flips, wholesaling, and creative simultaneous closings? I share the names of attorneys around the country who probably will close deals and/or know others who do. I also suggest contacting real estate associations for referrals.

I warn you, though, that you will find some Realtors who know nothing about wholesaling and lease optioning, renting to own, flipping, zero percent financing, brokering mortgages, and so on. These people belong to a group that says you can't do these things, because they have never done them themselves. Do not listen to them! It reminds me of my friend who has been divorced six times yet loves to give out relationship advice.

Another group of advice givers includes people who have failed miserably at something and love to tell you how bad the whole idea was. You may go to a real estate investor or a Realtor who bought a house one time, did not follow good policies and procedures, and lost money. They quickly tell you flipping will not work.

A third group that gives advice is made up of experts who have successfully worked in a certain field for years and years. They know exactly what they are talking about; they have encountered a full range of positive and negative situations. Listen to *them*. Make sure your advice comes from people in *this* category.

Everyone Makes Money

In the world of investing, you want everybody to make money. Actually, I like my clients to make a little more money than I do because the way to really profit in any business is have repeat clients.

Maybe I only make $8,000 to wholesale a property when I could have made $12,000. However, if my clients bought it from me, fixed it up, sold it, and made $30,000, they will come back. My lawyer friends have a saying: If you're going to rip someone off, do it once, do it big, and leave the country. Some real estate investors like to rip people off in little ways, and that is stupid! They don't make much money, and they have unhappy clients.

7. *Invest in your own home.* Your best real estate investment is your own home because you now know you can buy a home for less than what it is worth. Let me give you an example. You could buy a home worth $100,000 for $70,000. Instead of having a $100,000 mortgage, it will be $70,000 (or $68,000 with a $2,000 down payment). Your payment will be about $550 a month, depending on the interest rate. After living there for two years, you can sell it for up to $250,000, make a profit, and not pay any taxes on it (in the United States). If you're married, you can sell it for up to $0.5 million after two years or more.

Suppose that after two years, your home appreciates quickly and becomes worth $200,000. You find another deal, keeping the same level of mortgage payment but making money each time. That's tax-free income.

I believe that one of the best deals going is finding a good deal on your own home, living in it for about two years (check with your accountant for residency requirements), then selling it and making money tax-free.

CHAPTER 8

*Opportunity is missed by most people because it is
dressed in overalls and looks like work.*
—THOMAS ALVA EDISON

Do Not Pass Up These Sources of Income

This chapter discusses in detail several avenues of income introduced in Chapter 1.

Lease Options

A lease option means leasing a property with an option to buy it, commonly called *rent to own*. If you are leasing an apartment or a house now, you are always better off to own it. If you are an investor who has a property you want to rent, you are always better off lease-optioning it or setting up a rent-to-own situation, rather than just renting it out.

The statistics support this approach. According to various real estate groups around the United States, 97 percent of renters want to become homeowners but are not sure how, so a tremendous market exists for investors or real estate entrepreneurs.

For a comparison, let us look at the automobile industry. About 20 years ago, only two ways to buy a car existed: (1) pay cash, or (2) borrow money from the car company or your bank. Today, more than 50 percent of all automobiles are purchased through a lease option. In the luxury market, more than 60 percent of them are through lease option. That way, lessees put down a much lower down payment and make lower monthly payments than if they borrowed the funds to buy the car. At the end of two, four, or sometimes five years, they have the right to buy the car at a predetermined option price. Alternatively, they can give the car back to the dealer if it is not damaged and lease-option a newer one. It is a win-win situation.

In this country, an estimated 1 percent of all houses are lease option, so it is a wide-open market. You could learn to dominate this market in your area.

Controlling Property

Lease options are not only good for rental or rent-to-own properties, but they also provide an excellent way to control properties without using much of your cash or credit.

Suppose you found a beachfront condominium you could have either purchased or lease-optioned for $50,000 10 years ago that is worth $100,000, $150,000, or $200,000 today. If you had lease-optioned it for 10 years for $50,000, you could have purchased it within that time frame. (Lease option means you have the *right* to buy a home, but not the *obligation* to buy it.) Today you would either own it completely or sell it for a handsome (depending on the market) profit.

What results! Now, suppose every condo house in the neighborhood was available for lease option. How many could you lease option in the next 10 years for their investment value, knowing the market will likely go up? Do the math and you will see how lucrative this income source can be.

How Lease Option Works

To get started, find a fairly motivated seller. With lease optioning, unlike wholesaling, you do not have to find a supermotivated seller. The most profitable real estate deals require you to buy properties or put them under contract for 25, 30, 40 percent below current market value. That is, if you want to wholesale a property and it is worth $100,000, you need to purchase it for $65,000 to $70,000 so there is enough room for you to sell it and make a profit. If a seller says the property is worth $100,000 but he needs $82,000, many investors would walk away. With lease optioning and rent to own, however, you do not have to walk away, even at a moderate discount like $82,000.

The best way to find a motivated seller for a lease option is through the For Rent ads. Call landlords and property managers. If a property is for rent, do you think they might be motivated to lease-option it? Quite possibly they will be so motivated, and here's why: In the world of owning rental property, a For Rent ad signals that the tenant has vacated, probably leaving the place in a damaged state. It needs paint, cleanup, new carpet, and so on. In many cases, the tenant may not have paid the rent regularly, or neglected or damaged the property. The owner or manager likely had to drive back and forth to the property to make little repairs. With these hassles, the owner or manager is not likely making as much money as originally thought. He or she could simply be tired of managing it.

Fact-Finding Questions

When you call about the ad, write these questions down and have them handy when you talk to the landlord, owner, or manager.

1. *How many months has the property been vacant in the last two years?* The reply may be, "Someone moved out two years ago. It sat empty for two months. We rented to a couple who stayed for a year. Then it was empty for another month." So

out of the last two years, it was empty three months. If the rent was $1,000, that means $3,000 was not collected. Remember, real estate is numbers.

We have to present some powerful numbers to help convince the owner to go for a lease option on the property.

2. *How much money have you spent on repairs in the last two years?* This includes painting, cleanup, new carpet, appliance repair, and so on. The reply might be, "We painted it, and that cost $800. We had to replace the carpet a year and a half ago; that was $2,000. We did some yard work, which cost $500. We also did some work on the roof for $4,000. Oh, and the hot-water heater broke. That was another $800." Add up all those repair numbers.

3. *How much time do you spend worrying about the property, or going back and forth to it, or taking tenant calls every month?* The response might be, "It takes at least five hours for paper-work and answering the phone. When I have to lease it, I spend time driving back and forth to the property a lot." Add up those numbers.

4. *How much is your time worth?* If the response is $20 an hour and the answer to the previous question was, for example, eight hours, that is $160 more spent a month.

5. *What are the mortgage, taxes, and insurance costs?* When you total all the numbers defined through these questions, say, "When you subtract all the vacancy and repair costs, you are really only making about $650 a month and not $1,000." They will likely agree with you. You are leading up to making an offer.

Make an Offer

Start by asking this question: "How would you like to not have to worry about tenant repairs or tenant phone calls any more?"

The response will likely be, "That would be great. How do we do that?" Then ask, "How would you like to not worry about collecting rent money for the next five years? You just have to go to your mailbox and get your check. You don't have to worry about the property anymore." If you get a positive response, now offer the possibility of renting to own or lease-optioning the property to you.

You want at least a five-year lease at $650 a month (the actual intake). That locks in your cost for five years. (Maybe you will only get a 2-year lease, a 10-year lease, or more. You are limited only by your own creativity and ability to negotiate.)

Next, you offer to be responsible for the small repairs up to, for instance, $300. That covers 90 percent of those piddling repairs that drive landlords crazy. However, be clear in your contract that the owner is always responsible for big repairs over a specified dollar amount. In addition, you should carry insurance for any big repairs. If a storm damages the roof or the hot-water heater blows up, you have insurance to cover repair and replacement expenses.

The next step is to negotiate an option price by saying, "What is the absolute least amount you would sell or option this property for today?" If the response is, "The property is worth about $100,000, but I'd take $82,000," you would either accept it or keep negotiating. You point out it will probably take another 30 to 60 days to rent it and your first payment will not be due for 60 days. You explain that you are a professional real estate investor who will paint and do repairs and make payments regularly. In your disclosure, make it clear you do not represent them or their interests. Also be sure to disclose that you will sublet the property. Although the person still owns the property, you obtain the right to lease-option it for five years at the price you agree on. If money down is required, find out how much deposit is normally collected when the property gets rented. Ideally, your down payment should equal that amount.

However, you can even negotiate that. Point out that the tenant receives *back* the deposit money unless it is needed to pay for damages. As an alternative, suggest, "Since the deposit money belongs to the tenant and is really not your money, let me take that same amount of money and spend it making improvements over the next few months. You will be much better off because your property will be improved."

Once the lease-option agreement is signed, you control the property. Be sure to file that option document at the local courthouse to protect your interests so the owner cannot sell it out from under you. Both parties are protected that way. (Refer to Chapter 9 on asset protection for details.)

Move Forward to Make Money

Suppose that you have leased this property for $650 a month with the option to buy it for $82,000 within five years. It rents for $1,000 a month, and the market value is about $100,000.

Now that you control the property, you can move forward and make some money. The beauty of lease optioning is you really have four paydays. Here is how that works. You run an ad in the paper that says, "Rent to own. Stop throwing your rent money away. Become a homeowner. Easy qualifying." Do you think that would draw some attention and get some phone calls? Absolutely. Remember, about half of all real estate contracts fail because the buyers cannot get financing.

Your phone is ringing and people are saying, "I'd love to become a homeowner. I do not want to be a renter, and I'm tired of throwing my rent money away. I don't think I can buy, though, because I don't have a big down payment and my credit isn't perfect."

The first qualifying question you ask on the phone is this: "How much do you have to put down as option money?" Now, in your mind, you know you would prefer to have $3,000 down on a $100,000 house. That is three months' worth of rent. That will protect you against any vacancy or repairs. If someone calls up and says, "I have $8,000," what do you say? "We might be able to work something out." What if someone calls and says, "I only have $300 to put down?" You may not want to work with that person, because you do not have a big enough cushion to play with for this transaction.

> *Remember: Before you rent your property, always do a credit and criminal background check. Check with two previous landlords, and verify everything they have told you. Warning: Never give anyone a key to any of your properties if you have not done a complete credit and background check.*

Then ask them, "How much are you looking to spend a month?" Ask this as an open-ended question. If you say that $1,000 is what you need, they could respond with, "Great. A thousand's fine." However, if you ask, "What are you looking to spend?" and they reply, "About $1,100," you just earned a $100 rent increase. That's $100 a month times 12 months a year, which is $1,200—a $1,200 idea.

Payday 1. After everything checks out well on the background check, it is payday number 1. The tenants give you $3,000 option money up front. That is your money. You are not taxed on that option money until the option is exercised or a sale on the house closes. (That option money will go toward the purchase of the property, so you need to have access to it should they buy the property.) That is $3,000 in your pocket.

Payday 2. Your first payment is not due to the original owner for 60 days, and your new tenants are ready to move in 30 days. Now, take their $1,100 rent the first month, and you do not owe any payment for 60 days. You have payday number 2.

Payday 3. The tenants begin paying you $1,100 a month, and you owe the original landlord $650, so you are making a profit of $450 a month. At this point, you should be thinking, "How many lease options can I do?" How would you like to have 3, 5, or even 20 of these going every month?

Payday 4. Next, one of two things happens. You give the tenants an option for one year only to buy the property. They have 12 months to arrange a mortgage and buy the property. If it is $100,000 today, in 12 months (the term of the option), it could be worth $107,000. Always add a few dollars in because property generally appreciates in value.

Eight months from signing the lease-option agreement, one of two things will likely happen:

1. The tenant-buyers disappear in the middle of the night like some renters do. This is not necessarily bad! You can turn around and re-lease the property. Someone new offers another $4,000, $5,000, or $6,000 as option money. You start over again with your four paydays.

2. The tenant-buyers come to you and say, "We've gone to the mortgage company. We've been approved and we're going to buy your property." Many landlords get sad about this because they do not ever want to lose the property. However, that result is not as bad for an investor. They pay you $107,000, you pay the original owner about $82,500, and your profit is approximately $24,000 at closing. This is why you should not feel bad for yourself or any other landlord who has lease-optioned.

Give Rent Credits

Consider these nuances. First, always give some rent credit to the tenant-buyer. Maybe $100 to $400 a month of their rent every month goes toward the purchase price so your tenant-buyer can build a down payment. You need to escrow that money should they ever purchase the property.

Second, put in writing that the new tenant-buyer is responsible for all of the repairs up to the amount you agreed with the original owner (e.g., $300, $500, or $1,000). Also, explain that it is their home. They now rent to own it and are therefore responsible for repairs. This is important as most renters have no pride of owner-ship. Generally, when we rent a car, for example, we do not take good care of it, because it is not ours. If you instill in your tenant-buyers' minds that this is their home, that gives them incentive to take care of it, plant flowers, and so on.

Third, make sure that you have a separate lease and a separate option agreement in your documentation. If you ever have to evict your tenant-buyer, you need only the lease agreement when you go to the eviction court. Judges in eviction courts understand leases. A joined agreement that includes lease-purchase or rent-to-own doc-umentation could confuse the judge and weaken your case.

In Their Own Handwriting

Have you heard of Chinese torture techniques? In the Korean war, some of America's bravest, most patriotic soldiers were captured and led in front of television cameras where they were told, against their will, to speak badly about the United States. To get them to do this, the Chinese often used psychological torture techniques. Specifically, they discovered if they could get their victims to write down in their own handwriting certain statements, they could not deny them. The principle is this: You cannot deny what you have written in your own handwriting.

Therefore, in addition to using documentation for all of your tenant-buyers, get them to write these four points in their own handwriting:

1. "I understand I am responsible for the repairs up to the first $500."

2. "If I am late on any payment, I will lose all of my option money."

3. "If I do not close, refinance, and cash you out of the property within the next 12 months, then I will lose all of my option money and built-up funds."

4. "I promise to keep the property up to codes and to keep everything repaired as long as I am in the property."

So when the sink needs repair and your tenant-buyer calls and says, "Come fix the sink," you reply by saying, "Remember that handwritten paper you signed that said, 'I promise to keep everything repaired as long as I'm in the property.' Would you like me to send a copy of that paper to you?" I believe if people handwrote their own contracts, we would have fewer lawsuits. If your agreement were contested in court, the tenant-buyer might say, "I didn't understand this 10-page lease. It was too complicated for me." Then you produce a paper in his or her own handwriting that states "I'll lose all of my money if I do not pay the rent on time." How could the tenant-buyer argue then?

I recommend that you make sure every tenant-buyer writes out the key points of their contracts. Give them copies and attach these to the rent-to-own/lease-option contract.

Lease-Option Benefits

To summarize the advantages of lease optioning:

1. You can control a lot of property without using much of your own credit or money.

2. You can get out of the repair business, which can drive you crazy.

3. You can make money up front with option money differentials.

4. You can make money every month with the difference in rents.

5. You get big paydays when they close on the properties.

6. You can affiliate with a mortgage company and make it easier for tenant-buyers to get preapproved credit before the lease is ever signed.

7. You can help them start on a program to build up their credit so they can buy your property.

Summary of the Lease-Option Process

1. Find motivated landlords or property owners.

2. Walk these owners through the details outlining their actual earnings, assess the amount of time they spend on their properties, and find their pain in operating them. Determine if you can help them by taking the property off their hands at a discounted price.

3. Advertise and find qualified, hungry tenant-buyers who have cash to put down as option money, and who have good references and decent credit.

4. Make sure that the tenant-buyers understand all of their responsibilities for repairs and maintenance while encouraging them to take pride in their homes.

5. Affiliate with a good mortgage company so you can help your hungry tenant-buyers close on the property.

When the tenant-buyers do close on the property and you have a check in hand, I recommend congratulating them by giving them

---

Star Student

One of my students, Larry B. from Atlanta, Georgia, used this information to lease-option 14 executive homes in the $200,000 to $500,000 range. The average differential between rent money taken in and his costs was between $500 and $1,500 a month on each property—his profit. In the first year, three of the properties closed, so he made almost $100,000. Every time Larry closes a sale, he goes out and finds one or two properties to lease-option.

You can do a lease option with any type of property—vacation property, rental property, or commercial property. It is very powerful. It works.

flowers or arranging a limo ride to make them feel great about owning their home.

Questions and Answers

Q: What happens if you cannot rent the property? Do you have a way out with the original owner or landlord?

A: You can get creative and ask the owner to give you 60 days to get someone in the property. Put that request in writing and add a clause saying, "If I do not get a tenant, I can't go through with the deal." If your price and bottom rent are low enough, you should always be able to rent and market the property quickly, assuming you know the market. Do your research by talking to other property managers, investors, and landlords in the area to find out what the true rents are and how quickly things rent. Call on For Rent ads to see what the rents are and determine how long it takes to move a property.

Q: Who pays the insurance and taxes?

A: The beauty of renting to own and lease optioning is that the original owner still owns it. That person has all the liability and responsibility to pay for insurance and taxes. As you now have an interest in the property, be sure to get copies of that insurance, or even become named as the insured, which is easy to do. You also want to make sure the mortgage taxes have been paid, so ask for copies documenting that for every year you are involved in that property. Sometimes investors will take over a property, and the original owner stops paying the mortgage and taxes. It goes into foreclosure, and that causes problems for everyone. So make sure everything is current and stays current.

That is why you must disclose to your tenant-buyers that you may or may not be able to pass on a good title or that you may not have ownership of this property at this time. If anything bad happens to the deal, you have already disclosed it to the tenant-buyers to protect yourself. You may want to get your own insurance to protect against your activities.

Q: What is a fair commission to set up a lease option and flip it over?

A: Whatever you think is fair and whatever the deal will bear—the sky is the limit. I like to work backward and say, "There is $50,000 of profit in this deal. You'll make $50,000 if I do this deal. I should get at least $20,000 of it. If it is $600 a month, I should get at least $200. Or just pay me. You are going to make $50,000. Pay me $15,000 today and make $50,000 later." You can also use partnership equity sharing. (See the section titled "Partnering" in this chapter.)

Q: How do you conduct credit and criminal background checks on tenants?

A: Hire a professional firm and charge the prospective tenant-buyer an application fee, which pays for the expenses for the credit and criminal background check. (Go to www.shemin.com for names of good background- and credit-checking agencies.)

Q: How do you determine what that tenant-buyer can actually buy?

A: Remember, any time you consider selling a property to someone, get the person preapproved for financing. Put a system in place that allows tenant-buyers to work with your affiliated mortgage company to find out what they can afford before signing any paperwork.

Q: How do you know if a tenant or a tenant-buyer can afford to pay the rent every month?

A: Generally, the rent should be no more than one-third, or better, one-fourth of their income. If people want to rent an apartment for $1,000 a month, they should have $4,000 a month income. Unfortunately, many renters pay almost 50 percent of their income toward rent, so make sure that your applicants have a safe ratio in place before renting to them.

You can verify their income by getting current pay stubs and by checking with their employer, and, of course, using the background-checking agencies. However, I have some tenants who do not seem to work but who always pay their rent on time. If they put enough down and their track record is good, do you care?

Q: How many lease options would you like to have going?

A: How many do you think you could find? What type of property do you want to lease-option? Where? If you do not want to do it in your area, maybe there is a vacation area you want to be in. The main question is this: How many phone calls and how many For Rent ads are you willing to handle to find one lease option?

Generally, I make 15 to 25 calls and talk to 15 to 25 owners to find one or two lease-option potentials. Then I do my homework and make sure the numbers are as stated, verify the rents, and verify the market by talking to other professionals.

You can always run ads in the local newspapers. If you are doing executive homes, have an ad running constantly saying, "Rent to own executive home," and always have people calling you, so you are always having more tenant-buyers than you have property.

You can also advertise for acquiring rent-to-own property. "Landlords, sick of doing repairs? Tired of dealing with tenants? Let me help you out. Call now." You could do a free special report about how you are going to lease-option their property and get them out of all those repair headaches. You could have someone making phone calls for you. You can go make a presentation to a landlord association and see if you can get 10 properties all at once.

Q: What about property management companies?

A: You may call a lot of For Rent ads and get management companies on the phone. Some property management companies will work with you because they get a fee on the rent they collect. You can offer to take over the management of the property, control it, and pay the rent on time every month. They can collect their fee, and their repair costs will go down. However, you or the management company will need to talk with the owner to acquire an option to buy it.

Generally, when property management companies sell one of their owner's properties, they get a commission. You can offer the manager a commission if you have enough room in the deal. Do not let the fact that a property management company operates the property deter you from following through with your lease-option potentials.

Q: What kind of taxes do you have to pay as an investor when you sell a property?

A: If you buy and hold property, and your intent is to hold it for about a year, you can depreciate everything and write off the interest payments on your taxes. You also have some business expenses you might be able to write off. If you sell that property, generally the depreciation is recaptured, and you will pay taxes at the capital gains rate (about 20 percent) on your gain, plus the recaptured depreciation.

If you are wholesaling properties (i.e., putting them under contract and selling them), the Internal Revenue Service determines that you have a separate business, just as if you were buying and selling pictures, chairs, cars, jewelry, and so on. You pay ordinary income tax on it, plus about a 14 to 15 percent self-employment tax.

Often, investors, and especially beginning investors, talk themselves out of doing deals because they will have to pay taxes. Your goal should be to pay $1 million to the IRS because that means you made $3 million (if you fall in about the 30 percent tax bracket).

You can reduce your tax expense by, for example, incorporating your wholesale real estate business. This way, you can get extra benefits and write-offs and thus decrease the amount of tax you will pay on those activities. You can buy and sell properties in most cases through your self-directed IRA or do 1031 exchanges on your home properties and not pay taxes on them. Ask your tax advisor. These 1031 tax-free exchanges allow investors who have held property to buy new property of equal or greater value and not have to pay taxes on the gains. To learn how to save on taxes, go to www.shemin.com.

In my opinion, as long as the tax rate is below 50 percent, you want to make as much money as humanly possible and pay all the taxes you are legally and ethically bound to pay.

Q: Who do I need to have as advisors?

A: You need a team to be successful in any business, especially real estate: A good accountant (preferably one who owns real estate), a good attorney, a good mortgage company and banker, a good closing title company, some good repair people and contractors, and an excellent insurance broker. Always go to your team before you make any moves. Be sure to have them approve and make recommendations for fine-tuning your business plan, your money, and your tax planning.

Partnering

Another way to control property, make money, and not use any of your own credit is partnering. Remember, if you do not have the capital or credit or do not desire to use your own, get a partner to fund your business. It should never be a 50-50 partnership; someone has to be in control and make decisions, and that person should be you. Make sure you work with silent partners who do not interfere and tell you what color to paint the house, how much to rent it for, and so on. (About 70 percent of real estate partnerships fail because two equal partners cannot agree on anything.)

As a real estate investor, it can be difficult to borrow funds because you are self-employed and do not have much verifiable income in the beginning. You can overcome this by getting strong partners whose credit is excellent. Of course, you want to make sure that the deals you select are good and that your partners' interests will be protected. The numbers have to work.

Partners can provide lease-option money, wholesale properties, or buy and hold them. Make your agreement and split the profits in a fair way, usually 50-50. Do not let funding your business become a roadblock. Find a silent partner and share the profits.

A lot of people want to get into real estate but do not have time. If you have the time and the energy but not the money, you can put the deals together and partner with them. You can equally share in the monthly income and the profits when the property is sold or refinanced.

Also, with a partner funding your business, your name will not be on a lot of loans or deeds, therefore your liability will be low.

How to Attract a Partner

A young student of mine named Danny from Cincinnati, Ohio, wanted to create a business and bring in a partner to fund it. He put together a business proposal with a mission statement, pictures and descriptions of houses, and a statement of potential monthly profit. He visited with 45 potential partners and heard 44 no's, but the 45th person showed interest. A successful business owner, the partner was also a distant relative of Danny's. Together, they bought eight properties; each one cash-flowed $400 to $800 a month. They sold two of them within nine months and made about $35,000 profit on each one. Danny got one-half of that amount, or $17,500. His partner got tax write-offs on the properties to offset the liability against his regular income. He had put $100,000 into the investment properties and made 15 to 20 percent back—a good return using none of his own money because he had borrowed the funds. Today, they own more than 82 properties. Danny's net worth has reached approximately $5 million, and he is only 24 years old.

Partnering can work.

Be sure to put every partnership agreement in writing, disclose everything in writing, and have a protection clause that says something like, "There could be more expenses. We may not make as much money as we think. The property may not appreciate as we think." Think of every bad thing that could happen, put it in writing so both you and your partner are fully aware of it.

The best way to structure partnerships is through a limited-partnership agreement or a limited-liability corporation. If your partner wants to get all the tax deductions, title the properties in your partner's name, with you having a recordable interest. You could also put it in a land trust name to offer some liability protection. Please check with an attorney and accountant to ensure that your partnership structure and joint venture agreements are written in everyone's best interests.

Consulting Fees

If you put this information into action for the next six months or one year and do some deals like you should, you will become an expert, and then you will find, like I did, that everybody wants to take your time. People ask me often, "Robert, why did you write your first book?" The answer is that it was a complete accident. After I had about 20 properties, all of my friends, as well as strangers, started asking, "Robert, how do you buy all this real estate without using your own money? How are you doing these rental properties? You look like you are semiretired. Please tell me how to do it."

I was spending about 20 to 30 hours a week telling people the exact same thing. "Here's how you find deals. Here's how you contract them. Here's how you manage them. Here's how you make money." I wrote a report so I would not have to spend all of my time telling people how to do it, and I could go out and do the real estate and make money. Eventually, I realized that a person has only one asset in business: time. I therefore decided that if people want to use my time, I want to charge consulting fees.

Many successful Realtors now charge a small fee up front just to do business with buyers because often they drive around for three months showing 100 houses and buyers never purchase a property from them. If you are going to give people your knowledge and expertise, decide first what each hour of your time is worth. Then determine if you feel fair charging them. Again, only go forward charging if it is a win-win situation.

In the beginning, I gave away my ideas, and friends would buy 30 properties and make $500,000. I had consulted for free, and I felt good about it because I love helping people; however, please learn from this mistake of mine. You can actually charge consulting fees to help people get a house, help them rent to own, help them do wholesaling, and so on. After they get started, they could become excellent long-term clients. Consulting fees can be an excellent source of added revenue.

Be careful about the time you spend. Be aware of it and make sure you get paid for your time and expertise.

Contractor Referrals

On your team should be an excellent repair person or contractor, and as you deal with other investors, landlords, and tenant-buyers, they will ask you to refer good contractors and good repair people. You need to find some good ones who are referred, licensed, and bonded. You need to write up an agreement with those contractors stating that you will refer business to them in exchange for 5 to 20 percent of the total job cost.

Generally, in any business, especially with contracting, people take a percentage of their revenue—anywhere from 5 to 30 percent—

and spend it on advertising to get new business. You are giving them business they would not have had otherwise, so I think it is fair for them to give you a referral fee.

However, protect yourself by selecting referred contractors. Create a written agreement with the contractor stating how much and when you will be paid.

Make sure that you disclose to your clients two important things: (1) that you may or may not be getting remunerated or paid for referring this contractor, and (2) that even though you are referring the contractor, you in no way warrant or guarantee any of the work that the contractor may do for them. You always want to protect yourself in writing.

> *And one of the themes in this book—especially with real estate investing—is to have everything, every agreement and arrangement, disclosed to everyone in writing.*

Discounted Mortgages

Every time you come across another investor or landlord, ask, "Do you own or have any mortgages that you may want to sell immediately for cash?" If they do, get some basic information from them. (You can call my office at 1-888-302-8018, and we can give you excellent information.)

To buy a discounted mortgage, or to discount a mortgage and get paid for it, you will want certain things when you talk to the original owner of the note. You will need to obtain the following:

- A copy of the note that they want to sell
- The mortgage, deed of trust, or other security interest that secures the loan

- The settlement sheet that was given at the time of the closing of the note

- The payment records

- An amortization schedule, if available (if one is not available, we can create one)

- Any pertinent information about the property (e.g., What is it worth? What are the rents? What is the tax appraisal? What are the expenses?)

- Any title work that has been done on the property

- A copy, if available, of anything and everything that is recorded against the property

- A photo of the property, if available

Brokering Notes

Brokering discounted notes is an excellent business. If you find a note, for instance, that is $100,000, financed for 30 years at 10 percent interest, and that has been paid on for a while by a good credit-worthy customer, perhaps someone will only discount it and purchase it from you for $92,000, and you can offer the original seller $88,000. If it is accepted, you can make a profit of $4,000.

The note buyer handles all the legalities and the closings for you. You do not have to worry about that. You just find the notes and get offers on them. Then, of course, you have to sign the contract to buy the note; therefore, anytime you find a good note that someone wants to sell, you can broker it and make some profit.

People are profiting from brokering notes all the time—and you might as well be, too. It can be an entirely stand-alone business for you; however, I recommend it as a by-the-way business as you are calling on property owners, landlords, and investors. You always want to ask the magic question, "Do you own or hold any notes?" If the answer is yes, you ask, "Would you like to get some cash for that note now instead of waiting 10, 20, or 30 years to get your money back? Most often, the owners of the notes are interested in getting some of that cash.

■ A record of any improvements that have been made to the property since the original closing or since the original note was made

The more information you have, the better.

Renting Appliances, Furniture, and Cars

Over the course of the next 5 or 10 years, many successful real estate investors like yourself could come to own 10, 20, 30, 40, or even 100 properties. You could have a lot of tenants, tenant-buyers, and other investors. As in any business, you need to think about what else you can offer to your tenants, tenant-buyers, and other investors that you can profit from. Again, the most important thing is that you are offering quality services and quality products.

Let me just give you a rundown of how some real estate investors are making extra income and developing other income sources out of this business. For example, if you own rental property, I highly recommend that you get out of the appliance business. If you sup-

Good Example of Brokering Notes

One of my students, Susan C. from Manhattan, New York, found a commercial note that a seller had sold on an apartment building and taken back a first mortgage of $800,000. It was a 30-year note at 11 percent. The note purchaser, whom I helped to arrange the transaction, offered Susan $715,000, and she in turn offered the original seller $660,000. She made a profit of approximately $55,000 for just finding that one note. It took three weeks from the original first call she made to the actual closing, when she received her check.

Understand that the worse the credit rating and the worse the collateral, the less a note buyer will pay for a note. A second mortgage is harder to broker, and you get paid a lot less, if anything, because it is much riskier. Brokering notes can be an excellent by-the-way business, and it can become another source of income for adding thousands of dollars per month to your income through real estate.

ply refrigerators, stoves, and air conditioners, they are going to break and cost you a lot of money.

Instead of providing appliances, we refer people to a quality rental business. When a transaction takes place, we get a small referral fee. Again, all of our agreements are in writing, and we disclose them to our tenants.

We also recommend that our tenants carry renter's insurance, and we have a marketing agreement that is legal and ethical with an insurance broker. We get a small referral fee for that.

A lot of our tenant-buyers and tenants need furniture. We have also arranged to recommend a quality furniture rental place, and they likewise pay us a referral fee.

One day, I was at a fellow real estate investor's office when I noticed that the investors had seven cars sitting out in front of their office. These cars had For Sale signs in them. Often, they would buy these cars from their tenants who needed down payment money to buy one of their properties, or they would take the car of a tenant who could not pay the rent, or they would go out and find a great deal on cars (like you are learning to do on real estate). The real estate investors would then sell these cars on terms to some of their tenants who had good credit.

Cross-Marketing of Renters' Services and Products

If you can think of anything your tenant-buyers or other investors need, develop relationships with the appropriate suppliers and make a profit on the transactions. What other services or products could you repeatedly refer and realize a small fee?

Do other businesses operate in this manner? Yes. Every large apartment complex, most giant consumer companies (e.g., the giant auto companies), and hotel companies, among others, are always offering ancillary services. Whenever you stay in a hotel, they offer you Internet services. They offer you certain types of pizza delivery services and different items on which they likely collect revenue. They can offer about everything that their customers could want or need.

Likewise, the large apartment complexes share in the revenue from cable television, Internet providers, long-distance services, and so on. If they're doing it, why not copy what works to develop more sources of income for yourself?

CHAPTER 9

If I'd known I was gonna live this long,
I'd have taken better care of myself.
—EUBIE BLAKE AT AGE 100

Protect Your
Real Estate Assets

What interests successful real estate investors is not only making money, but protecting it. You can have many avenues of income from real estate investing, but if you are not careful about how you develop and protect them, you could lose them all. It is important to understand how to protect what you work so hard to get.

To protect what you have, let me tell you about problems you will face as a successful real estate investor. Then (do not worry) I will show you how to protect yourself against those problems.

Separate Asset Base (SAB)

Before we discuss asset protection, though, let me explain how you can get $1,051,694. Simply do this: From this moment forward, every time you make money (whether it is a check from your regular job, from wholesaling a house, from a lease-option deal, from a rental, from selling a house that you control, or from brokering a mortgage), take at least 10 percent of it and put it into a Separate Asset Base (SAB) account.

If you had been doing that for the last 15 years, where would you be today? And where will you be in 15 years if you take $375 a month—that is, about $85 a week—and invest it in a savings vehicle that earns you 11 percent? That vehicle could be discounted mortgages, real estate, or something else. If you can get an 11 percent return saving at a rate of $85 a week, you will have $1,051,694 in 30 years. If you were able to get an 18 percent return on that same amount of money, you would have $5,292,594 in 30 years.

One of the biggest mistakes people make in asset protection is putting all their eggs in one basket. A banker once said something I did not like: "The problem with you real estate people is all you have is real estate." He was right, though. I suggest you have more than one asset base, more than one source of income. Do that, but, most important, pay yourself first. Start doing that now through your SAB.

Getting Sued

About 30 million hospitalizations occur each year in this country, yet there are more than 120 million court filings every year. That shows you have three times more likelihood of going to court than going into the hospital. Average Americans will be involved in four to six lawsuits during their lifetimes, and these events make up the most likely reasons:

1. *Driving.* If you are in a bad car wreck and people get hurt and go to the emergency room or to intensive care for a couple of weeks, it can cost hundreds of thousands of dollars, if not millions, for medical care. Having to pay for that is probably one of your biggest risks.

   Do you have children? If they are under 18, you are responsible for everything they do. Maybe you are a good driver, but you cannot be with them all the time. They could get in a car wreck driving with others, and it will cost you. They could get in a fight, do something bad, and cause you problems. At the risk of sounding like a bad country song, if you are a livin', lovin', drivin', workin' person, you are always at risk of being sued.

2. *Your job.* You could do something wrong at work (sexual discrimination, for example). Maybe you are guilty, maybe you are innocent. Keep in mind, however, that you could get sued at work.

3. *Business relationships.* If you form real estate partnerships or other partnerships, you run the risk of getting sued.

Assess Your Risk

Ask yourself these two important questions: (1) What is my risk? (2) What are my assets that I risk losing? Realize that asset protection for someone who owns 20 hotels and 15 apartment buildings will be higher than for someone who just owns a broken car and has an overdue Visa bill.

To determine your level of risk, you need a financial picture of where you are right now. Fill out that financial statement we talked about in Chapter 2 (you can get them from a mortgage company or bank), and take a snapshot of where you are now. Sign and date it today and keep it for your records.

Judgments against You

In most states, judgments are good for 7 to 10 years and can be renewed indefinitely. So if you get sued and have a big judgment against you, though you may not own many assets today, you likely will in the next 15 or 20 years—owning a home or working at a high-paying job, for example. A plaintiff's attorneys will often wait 10 years or more to come after you if the judgment is high enough. So start thinking about asset protection today, even though you may not currently have any worries.

Also, if you get divorced and are obligated to pay child support, the courts could come after you—even put you in jail—if you do not pay as you agreed to pay. So start protecting your assets today.

Defenses for Asset Protection

What are some defenses or solutions to protect your assets? I will outline several here.

1. *Have subcontractors instead of employees.* You can cut down on the risks and hassles of hiring and managing employees by only hiring subcontractors in your business.

2. *Hire licensed, bonded, and insured contractors to do repair work.* If you do repair work yourself and install a faulty wire that burns down one of your houses and injures people, you could be sued. So make sure people doing your work are licensed, bonded, and insured.

3. *Do not drive a lot.* I actually bought a used limousine, and now I pay someone to drive me around because it saves me time (so I can be on the phone and make more deals), cuts down on my stress level, and is safer. Limousines rarely get into accidents because they are so big. It also makes me money because I rent the limousine on weekends to teenagers going to proms. It actually pays for itself! (By the way, I bought the limousine at a foreclosure for about 40 percent of what it is worth. My

10-passenger luxury limo cost less than a four-year-old Nissan Maxima.)

4. *Stop making people angry.* People who might sue you are generally angry because you did not treat them well. You did not return their phone calls or give them the services you promised. My advice is, do what it takes to make them happy. If your tenant is upset, spend an extra $50 and get the repairs done. Within reason, if you keep people from getting upset, they will not sue you.

5. *Simply stop owning things.* The more you have, the more you own, the more likely you are to get sued. Research indicates that if you earn more than $100,000 a year, you have a one-in-four chance of being named in a lawsuit. If you earn $250,000 a year, you have a one-in-two chance of being named in a lawsuit.

6. *Get assets out of your name.* That may sound silly, but most wealthy people do not put possessions in their own names. You may want to do the same if you are concerned about asset protection.

Ways to Protect Yourself

Let's look at three ways to protect yourself: (1) traditional asset protection, (2) trusts, and (3) proper insurance (your first line of defense).

Segregating Your Assets

Forming corporations and trusts helps you segregate your assets, which means getting assets out of your own name. Most people have their bank accounts, houses, and cars in their own names, so do couples. However, if you get sued, everything you own (that is in your name) can be attached by a judge to satisfy the suit. Depending on the laws in your state, if you are married and get sued, everything you both own is at risk.

Traditional Asset Protection

You can split ownership with your spouse, putting some items in your name and some in your spouse's. During the 1960s and 1970s, many well-to-do doctors put many of their assets in their wives' names. That meant if they got sued, they might lose their office equipment, for example, but not the large items they put in their spouses' names.

However, if you follow this traditional way, make sure your spouse will love you forever and never leave you. What if your home ends up belonging to the pool boy because your wife left you and married him? She could do just that if she owned the property.

Also be careful about splitting ownership among your children. When your children reach 18 and obtain title to your property, they may hate you and take revenge by taking over the property, even renting it to you!

Believe me, trusts, corporations, and perhaps partnerships are better ways to split possessions than this traditional way.

Two Types of Trusts

1. *Land trust.* Do you know that the worth of your home and debt owed is on public record when your home is in your name? Anyone, including a plaintiff's attorney, can find out what your property is, where it is, what it is worth, and what the debt is. To be anonymous, many people take their properties out of their names and put them into a land trust. Then you do not own it; the land trust does. You can call it the 123 Jones Street Land Trust and become the beneficiary, the owner, and the trustee. You control it and still get the tax advantages, but it is not in your name. Land trusts are also good if you are flipping, wholesaling, or lease-optioning houses. You can control them that way.

2. *Irrevocable trust.* This is a kind of trust you can set up, but you cannot change it because it is irrevocable. An irrevocable trust is almost impossible to break in any type of court or legal situation. If you have an irrevocable trust with $1 million of real estate that generates $100,000 a year and your child is the beneficiary, make sure it has a *spendthrift clause.* That will ensure that no one else (for example, a creditor who sues after a car wreck or a participant in a divorce) will be able to claim the money intended for your child. Also, if you have life insurance, your heirs might have to pay estate taxes on that life insurance. You can move that asset out of your estate and put it into an irrevocable life insurance trust. Remember, once you place your assets in an irrevocable trust, no one will be able to attach them.

Debt to Protect Assets

Another way to protect your assets is through debt. If you own 10 paid-for houses worth $1 million, would your assets look attractive to a plaintiff's attorney? Yes, of course they would. If you own 10 houses worth $1 million, but you also have $899,000 in debt,

---

Defining the Parts of a Trust

There are three parts to a trust: the agreement itself, the trustee involved, and the beneficiary or beneficiaries. They are defined as follows:

1. *The trust agreement.* Describes the agreement, what the trust does, who owns it, and what the owner's responsibilities are. It can say whatever you want it to say.
2. *The trustee.* The person who does what the trust agreement says. It can be you, an attorney, an accountant, or a trusted advisor. That person's only job is to do what the agreement says: manage the property, sign documents, pay bills, or whatever you specify.
3. *The beneficiary.* People who get the benefit of that asset. That could be you or your children, family members, or friends.

---

you become less attractive. I am not recommending going into debt, but it can be a viable asset protection tool.

Corporations and Partnerships

You can set up corporations and partnerships to help protect your assets. If you own assets and others sue you, they can get everything that is recorded in your name. If only a percentage is in your name and the rest belongs to a corporation, those suing you cannot get it all, only what remains in your name. A corporation or limited partnership is viewed as another entity by the law, separate from you, even though you still control its activities. For example, you might sell your equipment to your corporation and lease it back, so if you get sued, your equipment shows up as leased equipment, not an asset you own.

Most businesses in the United States operate through a corporation or partnership of some kind. These entities continue past your lifetime, they make you look more professional, and they allow you to run your real estate business with some level of asset protection.

You would choose from basically three types of corporations: S Corp, C Corp, and a new type called a Limited Liability Company (LLC). If you ask 100 attorneys and accountants which are the best states to incorporate in, most of them will say Wyoming, Nevada, or Delaware because these states seem to be in competition to outdo the others by making their corporate laws more attractive. If you ask 100 real estate attorneys what is the best way to own real estate, 90 of them will say a limited liability company. (Since lawyers will never agree on anything, 90 percent is excellent.)

LLCs offer these benefits:

- An LLC can do everything any other type of corporation can, in general.
- In many states, each limited liability company can have only one owner.

LLCs Keep the Best, Drop the Worst

The Limited Liability Company category was created to use the best of the other categories and leave out the worst. Some attorneys object to LLCs because they are new and untested in the law. However, they are statutory, and in most states, they are rock solid if you set them up properly.

- In certain states, an LLC can be set up anonymously.

- An LLC provides all the protections of every other type of partnership and corporation, and you can elect how you are taxed—either as a partnership or a corporation.

Can lawyers and plaintiffs bust open your limited liability company and get what is inside? Not if it is managed properly. All they can get is a charging order, which is what you, the shareholder, are entitled to. Here is an example of a charging order.

You control $1 million of real estate that produces $100,000 of income a year. The real estate is owned by your limited liability company. Someone sues you and wins a judgment against you. The plaintiff gets a charging order against the assets in your limited liability company—$100,000 a year. However, the rules of an LLC say you do not have to distribute income if you do not want to, so you tell the plaintiff's attorney, "Yes, we made $100,000 this

Work with Experts

I recommend you have an attorney experienced in your business completing your incorporation and partnership papers, plus making sure you follow through with the instructions every year. A lot of people file corporate forms but do not follow all the rules and file all the documents. If they ever get sued, their corporation can be torn apart because it is not valid. So *always* have professionals do your paperwork.

year and you have a charging order. The court says you have the right to this money, but we are not distributing it. According to the IRS, you will have to pay taxes on that $100,000, but you do not have the $100,000."

Do you see the value of *not* putting real estate in your name? If you had that million dollars of real estate in your name, the plaintiff could attach all of your real estate assets. Do you think anyone would want the tax liability for your limited liability company, but none of its assets or income? No. Do you think they would be willing to negotiate a better settlement with you? Yes.

So how do you want to hold your assets? How do you want to protect them? Take time now to look at the activities you are doing and decide the best way to hold them.

I always like to copy what successful real estate people do. Most large hotels and apartment buildings are owned by LLCs. I figure

LLC and Divorces

In a divorce situation (always a situation that poses one of the biggest threats to asset protection), an attorney friend of mine had a client, about 80 years old, who fell in love with a 25-year-old woman. The gentleman's net worth was about $30 million. (Of course, they only married for true love, but unfortunately became divorced soon after the marriage.)

The man's attorney had recommended he form a limited liability company, so when the woman sued her former husband for half of his assets, these assets could not be touched. The defendant's attorney said, "All you get is a charging order, and yes, we have earned about $2 million this year and you can get part of that, but you have to pay taxes on it, and we are not distributing any of the income. We are probably going to do the same for the next year, and the next year, and the next year. So you'll owe the IRS about $400,000 or $500,000 this year. Can you pay that?"

Not surprisingly, this couple worked out a more amicable divorce settlement.

that if it is good enough for their $50 million hotels, it is generally good enough for my little $50,000 or $80,000 duplexes.

> *If you acquire a lot of assets, have two or three different entities to sprinkle them in, so at no given time could they all be attached.*

If you are a drug dealer or an international terrorist, governments can likely get to your assets wherever they are. But as an investor, you can protect your assets if you set them up right. A successful investor friend named Bob owns nothing in his name. His cars are owned by one LLC; some of his real estate is owned by another. More of his real estate is owned by yet another corporation. He has trusts that own several liquid assets he controls. Because of his success, he has a lot of lawsuits against him. (I believe that if you are not getting sued, you are not doing enough business.) But no one can touch his assets because he does not own any of them personally—they are allocated among different entities.

Important Step: Record All Contracts

Whenever you sign a contract or option to buy a property, especially from a motivated seller, be sure to record that contract against the property at the courthouse in the particular town or city. In certain states, you can actually record the contract through an affidavit, which is basically a letter stating you have a contract or option on the property. That way, it is recorded and the whole world knows you have an interest in that property, so no one can sell or refinance it.

Insurance: First Line of Defense

Your first line of defense to protect your assets is insurance. If something happens to your home, you have home, fire, and some liability insurance. If something happens to your car, you have vehicle insurance. I suspect you currently do not have enough car insurance, maybe a standard $300,000 or $500,000 policy. But if someone gets in a bad car wreck and goes into intensive care for

Lesson Learned about Recording Contracts

I once put a house, which was worth about $80,000, under contract for $50,000. The seller was highly motivated and happy to sign the contract. I lined up a buyer for $65,000 and stood to make about $15,000 on the deal.

A week later, I called the seller to make sure everything was OK, and he said, "Robert, I'm sorry. I've already sold the house." I replied, "How could you do that? You signed a contract with me." He said, "Someone else came along and offered more, so I just sold it."

I found out whom he sold it to and called that buyer. I said, "You can't buy that house. I had it under contract." He cussed me out and said, "Call my lawyer." When I talked to the lawyer, he laughed and said they just closed on the deal that morning. So I raced to the courthouse and learned they had not filed the deed yet. I recorded my contract against the property before they recorded their deed, thus creating what is called a "cloud on the title." That meant the officials could not pass title for that property until the cloud was cleared up.

Then I called the lawyer back and said, "When you do a title search, you'll see that my contract was recorded before your deed." The phone went silent for about three minutes and then he quietly asked, "What do you want?"

In this case, the seller had sold a house he did not have clear title to. The title company had even written title insurance on it. So now, not only was the seller in trouble, but so were the lawyer and title company, who all knew about my contract. As a result, I made a good wholesale fee on that property.

The fees to record property differ for each county and recording office. It is well worth the cost to record your contract, as this example shows. I highly recommend it.

two weeks, for example, hospital bills could easily exceed $300,000. That is why I recommend getting an umbrella policy.

Umbrella Policy

An umbrella policy generally costs between $10 and $20 extra a month for an additional $1 million of coverage. It covers your car and home, and may include up to five rental properties. Please check with your insurance broker about umbrella policies. They are affordable and offer extra protection.

Managing Property Insurance

Call your insurance broker and find out if you are insured for all the activities you are doing. The most active suits in the United States right now are directed at property managers. So if you manage property, ask about special insurance to protect against property management lawsuits. At the very least, make sure you are properly insured and perhaps incorporated as well.

Workers' Compensation

If you are building houses and running repair crews, make sure you are insured for those activities. A big hole in a lot of real estate investors' protection plans is not addressing workers' compensation. If the repair people who regularly work for you get hurt and have no coverage, they could sue you, the real estate investor.

If people work for you three to five days a week and you direct their activities, the courts could deem them to be employees even though you have subcontractor agreements with them. Make sure they have workers' compensation insurance and, if they do not, carry a policy that will cover them.

Ultimate Asset Protection

If you get sued, you run the risk of having your bank accounts and real estate holdings attached. Not only can the plaintiff's attorneys take this action, but so can government agencies. They could keep you from selling assets until all charges have been resolved. It is called a *lis pendis*. They can file a *lis pendis* against your property in certain instances, thus making it difficult to operate if you do not have access to your cash, your capital, or your assets.

Going Offshore

One of the ultimate asset protection tools is keeping your assets offshore. If your assets are in the United States, they can be reached eventually, even if they are part of a corporation or trust. It is possible that a plaintiff's attorney can bring you into court, do depositions, and make you reveal where your assets are, including

Do What Is Best for Your Situation

Remember, with any asset protection tool, you are always weighing the advantages against the disadvantages. By incorporating and using trusts, you get anonymity protection, but you also have to do more paperwork and more bookkeeping. They can be complicated and costly since fees are involved. I am always buying, selling, and refinancing. I like to keep things simple; so do the banks and title companies. To minimize confusion, I keep some properties in my own name and I carry adequate insurance.

Here are examples of the approaches two investors take. John C. has 42 properties and is always flipping and lease-optioning more. Someone sued him, got a judgment, and attached all the properties in his name so he could not sell any of those properties without first paying the judgment.

Another investor, Howard, owns about 80 properties. He placed 20 in one LLC and 20 in another. He also put a few in trusts. If someone gets a judgment against him, only the few houses still in his name could be attached; the ones he put in those corporations or trusts cannot be attached. He continues to buy, sell, and refinance without having to worry about judgments because of the way he set up his corporations.

So you need to determine what your risks are, what your activities are, and what your tolerance for paperwork is. The more complicated you make your asset protection, the more complicated your life will be. And, as with everything in finance and real estate, make sure you deal with referred, competent professionals concerning any aspect of asset protection.

offshore. Going offshore makes your assets difficult (if not impossible) to find. Keeping them offshore may also bring some tax advantages, though if you are a U.S. citizen, you are required to report worldwide income on your tax return. Remember, not reporting your income is illegal.

So much money has gone offshore that some of the states have created quasi-offshore accounts. I am not recommending it for everyone, but it could be an alternative for you.

The events of September 11, 2001 have dramatically changed the nature of offshore holdings. Because of international terrorism, the United States has put tremendous pressure on all foreign banks, making it more difficult than ever to open an offshore account. Owners of accounts already in place are required to disclose a tremendous amount of information to the authorities because governments and financial institutions are searching for people hoarding money illegally and doing illegal acts in this era of fear.

If you have a legitimate business purpose in opening an offshore account, you can still do so, but you have to be willing to go through all the steps.

CHAPTER 10

Understanding human needs is half the job of meeting them.
—ADLAI STEVENSON JR.

Legal Protection *and* Another Income Source

When you develop various sources of real estate income, you worry about protecting them, so you want to work with good lawyers. I found Pre-Paid Legal Services, Inc., which I have used almost weekly for the last several years.

For Clarification

The information included here about Pre-Paid Legal Services, Inc., is a general overview. Please remember that only the plan contract and associate agreement can give actual terms, coverage, amounts, conditions, and exclusions.

You can find an attorney on your own who may or may not be good and who will charge you anywhere from $150 to $300 an hour. However, Pre-Paid Legal Services, Inc., will help save you a lot of money on attorney's fees and also give you the ability to contact top attorneys in any area of the law you need.

I am an independent associate with Pre-Paid Legal Services. I became involved with this company a few years ago and now market its services. Pre-Paid Legal Services is a New York Stock Exchange company. Available all over the United States and Canada, Pre-Paid Legal Services has been in business for more than 30 years (so the organization must be doing something right). Many different people—magazine columnists, professionals, experts—are recommending this organization. *Forbes, Fortune, The Wall Street Journal, HR, Human Resource,* and almost every major business and insurance publication have, in the past few years, reported on Pre-Paid Legal Services, Inc., favorably. As a matter of fact, the American Bar Association has published a quote that says, "Americans have come to view legal assistance as a necessity. The best way for the majority of Americans to be able to assure themselves of legal assistance when they need it is through a prepaid legal plan." Notice the quote says, "the best way." That is a powerful statement.

Basically, every legal need you have ever had, do have, or will have is covered under featured aspects of the Pre-Paid Legal plan. There are five areas of coverage, plus some bonuses. (The following reflects my views about Pre-Paid Legal Services, Inc., and not necessarily those of the company.)

Preventive Legal Insurance

For a small monthly fee—generally $26—you, your spouse, and your children (through college age) are covered for legal fees in the United States and parts of Canada.

Especially if you are a real estate investor, you will want to ask lawyers a lot of questions. "What do I do if my tenants do _____?

What is the lease-option rule? What should I do when I am having trouble with my contractor? How do I collect money owed to me? What do I do when the bank does not treat me fairly? Is the information the mortgage company told me accurate?" Any time you have legal questions, you can call your Pre-Paid Legal attorney and get answers. Whatever is on your mind—a simple $50 problem or a complicated $500,000 problem—pick up your phone. You get almost unlimited telephone consultation for personal or business questions. Yes, both personal and business.

If you do not have a prepaid legal plan and call an attorney, an hour-long consultation will likely cost you between $100 and $300. With Pre-Paid Legal Services, Inc., if you call and ask questions, your legal bill is simply $26 a month.

If your attorney deems it necessary or appropriate, he or she will write a letter or make a phone call on your behalf. If your car does get not fixed properly, for example, and you call your Pre-Paid Legal law firm, your lawyer there would write the repair shop on the firm's stationery demanding the shop make the situation right. "Fix this car . . . pay her the money . . . finish the paint job" or whatever the issue. Most law firms would charge a lot of money for that, but Pre-Paid Legal Services, Inc., covers it.

Sometimes people say, "Robert, I don't like attorneys very much. I don't use them. I don't want to use them. I don't need this service, even though I heard it is a great company and they have great attorneys." Then I ask this: "Have you in the last year or two, or will you in the next year or two, sign any contracts or documents?

Where Would You Be without Health Insurance?

You may be asking, "What kind of attorneys do I get for $26?" After all, it is an insurance-type program, a pooled program. So I ask this question: If you have health insurance, how do you expect to afford a good surgeon for $200 a month? It is the same with legal services.

Will your family sign any contracts or documents?" Buying a car, borrowing money, buying a house, employment agreements, lease agreements, health club agreements, cell phone agreements? Who wrote all those contracts and documents you sign? Attorneys. *Their* attorneys, not yours. So you actually are involved with attorneys all the time, but they do not represent your interests.

People in wealthy families say, "Let me run it past my law firm," before they sign anything. After you sign up for Pre-Paid Legal Services, Inc., you can send your contracts (up to 10 pages, unlimited personal issues and a few business issues a year) to a law firm in the program and have a lawyer review your paperwork.

Comprehensive Will

The first thing Pre-Paid Legal Services, Inc., does for its members is handle writing a comprehensive will. (If you do not have a will, you are not alone. Eighty percent of Americans do not have wills either.) A top estate-planning attorney charges $500 to $1,000 to write up a will, and charges even more for people with complex estates. The company immediately takes care of the will of the member as part of the $26 per month fee.

If you want strangers to decide where your children and your possessions go at your death, then do not get a will. If you care, then you absolutely need one.

A $450 Embarrassment

When I was buying a used car, I looked at the contract (I am an attorney, you see) and said, "It looks fine to me." But I decided to fax it to my Pre-Paid Legal Services, Inc., law firm because this service was already paid for. A lawyer looked at the contract and said, "Robert, this is a used car. They're charging you a $450 destination charge. There is no destination if you buy a used car." I felt embarrassed but was glad he saved me $450.

How many contracts are you going to sign in which you will fail to catch something important? Let experts at your law firm review them, too.

On a Will-Writing Mission

I confess that I am involved in Pre-Paid Legal Services, Inc., because I have a mission . . . to get everyone to put together a will.

I often speak in front of groups and present Pre-Paid Legal as an employee benefit to a lot of small, medium, and large companies. A while ago, I presented to a group in Nashville, Tennessee, and one of my friends from high school attended the meeting. Of about 30 employees there, most of them signed up for Pre-Paid Legal that day because they saw its value and wanted to get their wills done.

However, my friend did not sign up, so I asked him, "You're married and have two children. Why don't you get your will done?" He replied, "I'm going to think about it." I said, "What's to think about? It's a $26 a month with a one-time $10 sign-up fee. Get your will done. If you don't want to continue the service, you are not locked in. Just get your will done."

Six weeks later, while he and his wife were still thinking about it, they were driving around town. They had stopped at a red light and a drunk driver ran the light, rammed into their car, and killed them both. The two sets of grandparents cared deeply about the children, but unfortunately, the children had to go into the custody of the state because the parents had no will to express their wishes.

I had some associates who never thought disaster would strike, but they perished when the World Trade Center collapsed in September 2001. I had told them many times, "Get your will done. Sign up for Pre-Paid Legal Services, Inc.," and they did not do it. Their estates are now in big trouble because they did not have the basic document that would have protected their assets—a will. Everyone needs to have one. Get your will done, please! Pre-Paid Legal Services, Inc., will make your will for you and even review it once a year.

Represent You in Court

Once you have been a member of Pre-Paid Legal Services, Inc., for 14 days, if you get a speeding ticket (or your teenager does) anywhere in the United States, the company will send a lawyer to court for you in most cases. Now, these lawyers cannot get your tickets thrown out for you, but they can go to court for you and plea to get your points reduced. The bonus is that you do not have to miss work while the lawyers work for you.

Do you have a big hole in your insurance program? Find out today. If you are criminally charged (like with manslaughter or vehicular homicide), your car insurance will not pay for your defense but Pre-Paid Legal will. Assuming you were not high on drugs or alcohol when the accident happened, this service will provide unlimited defense—win, lose, or draw. If you are worried about being named in a civil lawsuit, you should be. It could happen and, if you are not a Pre-Paid Legal Services member, you will have to find an attorney, pay a retainer fee, and defend yourself—whether you have done anything wrong or not. When you sign up for Pre-Paid Legal Services, Inc., you automatically have 75 hours of top attorney time a year to defend or consult with you. Go to www.prepaidlegal.com for full details.

Prepaid Legal and Taxes

When it comes to taxes, as a Pre-Paid Legal Services, Inc., member, you will receive 50 hours of tax attorney time if you are named in an IRS audit on your personal tax return. You can also call your tax attorney and ask tax-related legal questions as you prepare your taxes.

If you are dealing with a legal issue outside of the regular covered services, Pre-Paid Legal will give you a discounted price when you

What Is Coverage Worth?

What is 75 hours of top attorney time worth? It may not get you a trial as big as O. J. Simpson's, but it will get you a good start. It might be worth $15,000, $20,000, or $30,000 of attorney time in the bank. Every year you remain a member of Pre-Paid Legal Services, that benefit increases. After five years as a member, I have 335 hours of top lawyer time (even though I have been named in some little civil lawsuits because I do a lot of business).

do need to pay a lawyer's fees. In my state, instead of $200 or $300 an hour, Pre-Paid Legal Services, Inc., has negotiated a discount to $95 an hour. Other firms may charge you 50 percent of their normal fee.

Top Law Firms

Of your $26 a month, a good portion pays for lawyers. Pre-Paid Legal puts out millions of dollars each month to top law firms whose lawyers are happy to answer your questions and do your wills. This system *attracts* excellent law firms. All firms in the network are rated A, B, C, or D. An A rating means the firm performs in the top 5 or 8 percent of all law firms. In most states, Pre-Paid Legal Services, Inc., only uses A-rated attorneys and their firms. That means they are the biggest and best, and they offer full service.

Can they do real estate law? Can they do divorce law? Bankruptcy law? Criminal law? Tax law? Insurance law? Yes, they are the biggest, best law firms around the country, and you can have access to them.

Legal Access 24-7

Included in that $26 per month is 24 hours a day, seven days a week access to attorneys. (It's available in most states. Services do vary from state to state, so read Pre-Paid Legal brochures and contracts carefully.) If you were ever pulled over, detained, questioned, or arrested by the police, you could reach a lawyer to get help.

The police have a tough job. Most of them are great people, but if they pull my car over in the middle of the night, I am scared because I do not always know my rights. Do I have to answer their questions? Can they look in my trunk? Do I have to tell them if I was doing something wrong?

Legal Shield

Maybe you feel that you get treated differently because of the way you look, the color of your skin, the car you drive. All of a sudden,

Pre-Paid Legal Services, Inc., puts into your hands a legal shield for you and your family. If your teenagers, for example, get pulled over by the police who want to question and detain them, and they show their membership card indicating they have immediate access to top attorneys, they might be treated differently.

I would not let any of my loved ones drive around without that legal shield, because we all have Constitutional rights, even if we may not be aware of them. I highly respect this company and its chairman for creating this legal shield to make sure that everybody is treated fairly because of this access to top attorneys.

Legal Business Advice

For your business, you can call and ask questions about incorporation procedures, LLCs, limited partnerships, real estate contracts, lease options, tenant problems, collection problems, credit problems, even divorce and bankruptcy problems.

If you would like more information about Pre-Paid Legal Services, Inc., go to my web site at www.shemin.com.

Pre-Paid Legal Services as a Source of Income

Basically, I got started in Pre-Paid Legal Services while making real estate deals, talking to other investors, and getting to know landlords and property managers. As we talked, I would say, "By the way, I found this really great service." I would pull out a brochure and an application (even though I was not selling the service at the time). I just saw it as valuable. Then I found out I could actually turn these recommendations into a business as an independent associate.

Pre-Paid Legal Services can even be another income source for you. Becoming a sales representative requires going through training and sticking with it so you can make it work for you. If you are interested, we will work with you using our resources and Internet training as well as training and meetings in most major cities. In addition to hosting conference training calls, we also sponsor weekly and monthly events for yourself and your guests. As an associate, you can get access to our beautiful multi-million-dollar web site, which becomes *your* site and allows you to sign up new members online.

How the Business of Pre-Paid Legal Services, Inc., Works

First become a member of Pre-Paid Legal Services, Inc., so you can experience the services firsthand. Then become an independent associate, working both for yourself and within this large organization. You are the boss, so you can make your own business as large or as small as you want it. When you join my group (go to www.shemin.com for details), we support you in whatever way we can.

You can easily start by selling individual memberships one on one, as I did in the beginning. Commissions start at about $75 per membership. For example, if you interest people through the brochure and they go to your web site, or you give them a tape or video and they sign up for the service, you will get a commission of about $75 per membership. That amount goes up once you sell a certain number of memberships. Please read the actual agreement on my web site (www.shemin.com).

You can go into mainly small- and medium-sized companies to enroll 20 to 100 people at a time. Pre-Paid Legal Services, Inc., is one of the hottest employee benefits going. Across the country, we are uncovering a huge demand for Pre-Paid Legal Services and we have penetrated only 1 to 2 percent of the market.

You can get paid for training and developing a sales force *and* make overrides on what they do, just like any other sales business does. Pre-Paid Legal Services has a sales commission plan similar

The RICH Formula

Stop trading your hours for dollars. Real estate investing is one way to do that; so is Pre-Paid Legal Services. This is because it can make you RICH. Remember that term? Residual Income Creates Happiness.

I have met people who still receive residual income checks and have not sold a membership in 10 or 12 years. If you are interested, go out, get trained, work hard, stick with it on a part-time or full-time basis, and develop a small, medium, or large residual income down the road.

to those of most finance and insurance companies in this country. You can make a great part-time or full-time income. Some people develop large national sales forces and make *overrides* that are substantial.

Questions and Answers

Q. What do you get for the fee you pay to be an associate?

A. When you pay the one-time fee of about $249, you get trained in the product and receive sales materials. You also get a home study course and access to a local fast-start training class.

Q. How well can you expect to do financially by going into Pre-Paid Legal Services, Inc., as a business?

A. Let me first give you a comparison. A friend of mine just bought one of the top franchises in the United States, a retail store. He spent $120,000 on that business. In his first year of operation, he plans to make between $10,000 and $20,000 working six days a week. He mortgaged his house and is $90,000 in debt, so you can see he is serious about the business. In the second year, he will make $30,000 to $40,000; in the third year, $50,000 to $80,000. In the fourth or fifth year, he might sell it and pocket $200,000.

Just as in most businesses, including real estate investing, most people who become involved do nothing. The people who do nothing are paid nothing; the people who do little are paid little; and those who do a lot reap commensurate rewards.

The investment for Pre-Paid Legal Services, Inc., is a one-time fee plus (in about 14 states) a fee of about $130 to get a license to sell. Personally, I think it is too low. If the fee to sell these services was $30,000, some serious people would still step forward.

If you come in for $249 and sell five memberships, you would bring in about $500. That puts you in the profit zone immediately. If you sell five to seven memberships a month for a year, you can earn trips to exotic locations and a car allowance of about $300 a month besides the commission.

I'm sold on this program both as a service and as another source of income. I encourage you to look into this today at www.shemin.com.

Please consult company brochures and contracts, because commissions, coverages, and bonuses may change.

CHAPTER 11

It's the constant and determined effort that breaks down all resistance and sweeps away all obstacles.
—CLAUDE M. BRISTOL

Systemizing Your Avenues of Income

The problem for most real estate investors, including yourself, is the wonder and worry. How do I do this? What am I supposed to do? How am I going to react to this situation? What if this happens? What if that happens?

Operate your real estate business and your various sources of real estate income like every other successful business. Have policies and procedures and, therefore, make no decisions.

When I began in real estate, I used to worry about every little decision. "She can't pay the rent. He can't pay the rent. Should I buy it? Should I not buy it? How do I lease it? How do I find another buyer? Should I refinance this? Should I wholesale it? Should I

1. Write out your policies and procedures before you even begin looking for properties and contracting them. Define, for example, what a good deal is to you. What percentage would it have to be so it is worthwhile to you?
2. Put that good deal under contract immediately, with contingencies.
3. Start advertising and contacting your list of potential good buyers the day you put it under contract.
4. Make it your policy to decide who can you call immediately to get an answer if you run into a roadblock. Perhaps it's a real estate accountant, a real estate attorney, or a real estate escrow person. Perhaps it's someone on your team, like your banker or real estate broker.

flip it? Should I lease-option it? Is it a good deal? Is it not a good deal?" However, especially as I get numerous sources of income going, I answer these questions by just sticking by the policies and procedures I set.

Let me share some of my policies. Use them, add to them, or copy them as you wish.

Standards for Rental Property

Have written minimum standards that do not discriminate based on race, creed, color, religion, sex, family status, or disability.

Some of my written minimum standards for my renters or lease-option tenant-buyers are that they:

- Have two good references from two previous landlords.
- Have at least three times their rent as disposable income.
- Pass a credit and criminal background check.
- Are honest and pleasant.

- Have an emergency fund or available credit of some sort.

- Have stayed in previous rentals at least a year and a half, or have a very good reason why they moved out early.

- Pay the full deposit. (We keep advertising for the space until we get the deposit.)

- Don't go into a rental unit until it is absolutely ready to be rented.

Also, we assign numbers to the applications we take over the phone and in person, then rent to the first qualified renter that meets our written minimum standards.

Policies for Collecting Rent

Rental collection laws and tenant laws vary in every state, so check with your attorney before you use the following as your own policies and procedures.

- Rent is due on the 1st. Renters have to pay a late fee on the 5th. Eviction for unpaid rent begins on the 13th. No exceptions.

- We offer a rental discount program. If we want to collect $1,000, we say the rent is $1,100, and it will only be $1,000 if they pay by the 1st.

- When tenants have trouble paying the rent, we give them a list of local nonprofit groups and governmental agencies that can assist them.

- We give tenants a list of what repairs cost that they're responsible for, so if they do any damage, they know it will cost up front. We have them sign the list when they move in. For example, if it costs $30 to replace a window, the list says the cost is $60; a $50 plumbing repair costs them $100. Unpaid repairs or damages by tenants become unpaid rent. We will evict. Make this a profit center.

- If tenants say they want to move, we have a retention program and we call to find out why they are leaving. If they are good tenants, we try to talk them out of moving. It saves anywhere from $800 to $1,500 per unit if they stay. It's called our "save" program.

- We reward tenants who renew their leases by offering a gift worth $30 to $100 (for example, a free carpet cleaning, ceiling fan, or brass kick plate). If they stay three years, we offer them a free appliance, like a refrigerator or television. It only costs us $100 but is well worth it to keep our tenants.

Finding Good Deals

These policies keep our pipeline to good deals active.

- We make at least 20 to 50 phone calls a week looking for good deals.
- We develop relationships with mortgage companies, finance companies, and other professionals involved in foreclosures. We contact them biweekly to let them know we are looking for properties (either through a phone call or a letter or both).
- We immediately get an owner or seller on the phone and fill out our property acquisition sheet (it states what we can get the property for, cost of repairs, current market value, comparable sales, mortgage to be paid, reason for selling, length of time on the market, how much they bought it for, and how long they have been trying to sell it). If it sounds like a good deal with at least 25 percent profit margin, we put an offer on it and get a contract signed once we feel comfortable with the numbers.
- When an offer is signed, within that business day we begin marketing it to people on our list of potential buyers by making a flyer and calling.
- We never set a price on the property but let the market determine price by asking potential buyers, "What would you pay for this property?"

- When someone wants to put an offer on any of our properties, we never sign it unless the prospective buyer is preapproved and can show written proof of the preapproval or availability of cash to close the deal.

General Business Policies and Procedures

- Return all phone calls within one business day. If people call in the morning, make sure their calls are returned by that afternoon. If they call late in the day, make sure they are called by the next business morning. The biggest frustration potential sellers, tenants, and buyers have is that no one calls them back. The average telemarketer can make anywhere from 20 to 60 calls an hour, so we can call everybody back within that business day, and so can you.

- Set a three-day repair guarantee. If we don't fix our tenants' repairs in three business days, we give them their daily rent back in cash. That shows we are serious about repairs and want to take care of our tenants.

- Touch all mail only once.

- Touch all paperwork only once. Like the mail, open it and immediately act upon it or put it where it needs to go.

- Pay all bills upon receipt.

- Have one folder for each property. Take a photograph of each property and place it in the folder.

- Always pay people bonuses if they do a good job. If we promise $500 to someone who bird-dogged a deal for us and we make a lot more than that, we pay them a bonus above the promised amount.

You can add to these policies and procedures as you go along, but I guarantee having them will cut down on your stress and worry.

For instance, when you use that rent collection policy, you no longer have to worry about when to collect rent or when to evict someone who does not pay. It reduces your stress and worry because you can say, "You know, Mr. and Mrs. Tenant, I wish I could say you didn't have to pay the rent, but the policy and procedure of our company is this [and state the policy]. That's all we can do." Now, you have no stress, no worry.

Ethics and Your Real Estate Income

To get into real estate investing, all you need are properties and contracts. But, like every industry, real estate investing attracts great people and can also attract liars, cheaters, and crooks. So always protect yourself from them by verifying everything in writing, only working with people you know and trust, and only working with people who are referred to you, especially in the contract area, the mortgage area, and the other professional services areas. If you're not 100 percent comfortable doing a deal or dealing with someone, don't do it. Move on. Following this advice will save you a lot of headaches.

Some people think you can make money by ripping others off. That may be true, but you also feel bad. Besides, it is most often illegal and unethical. If you do it, you won't be in business very long.

Get Organized

Please do not operate your real estate business like I did the first two years, using yellow stickies on my car and stuck to the side of my desk. Get organized from the start. Make sure your bookkeeping, accounting, banking, and filing systems are set up to do your real estate business.

These days, you can do most everything on the computer using Quickbooks. It's an inexpensive program with lots of different functions and accounts. It actually has a section set up for real estate to make your job easier.

You also want to open up one bank account for each of your real estate avenues of income. Do not commingle your funds. For example, if you have rental property, have a separate accounting system and dedicated bank account for it. If you do wholesaling and flipping, have those transactions in a separate entity with a separate accounting system and bank account. If you're out discounting mortgages, put that under a separate accounting system, separate filing system, and separate bank account.

Get someone who is proficient in bookkeeping or accounting to set up your system now. Real estate can be a lot of fun and profitable, but it also can be a tremendous amount of paperwork, especially as you start doing more and more deals.

Filing Ideas

You should always keep certain files for all your activities. Here are some recommendations:

- Keep a file just for potential deals that you can go back through, and back through, and back through, with your property acquisition sheets.
- Keep a folder on each property with the address on the top and a picture.
- Keep all of your incoming and outgoing bills separate, so you know what to pay and what's going in and out.
- For every closing that you do, make sure you receive all the paperwork. Have a checklist so that you know you are getting the original filed closing statements, deeds, notes, and title insurance. Also make sure they give you amortization schedules, so you know what the loan balances are at all times of all the debt that you or your partners may have. Being organized now will help you tremendously in the future.

Get Help from Experts

If you're not good at something, get help doing that, even paying your bills. By paying a bookkeeping service just about $100 a month, I ensure that all my books, records, and financial statements are clear and legible. At the end of the year, all my tax work is done because the bookkeeping or accounting firm has kept good records. You may want to consider doing the same. That frees you to find more deals and make more money. It is also liberating when a bank or partner needs a copy of your financial statements or balance sheets. You can find them easily, and they will be professionally done.

Productivity and Time Management

If you are out finding good deals, your hourly rate will be in the hundreds, if not thousands, of dollars. Beware of spending lots of time on activities like dealing with contractors, driving to the paint-and-hardware store, taking tenant calls, trying to collect money, and running errands. These time-consuming, stressful, and nonproductive activities hurt your real estate investing business. Consider these ideas:

- Keep track of the amount of time you spend in half-hour or quarter-hour increments in your real estate business. Keep a daily log, a weekly log, and a monthly log. Every week, find out how you spend your time and what makes you the most money for the time spent. Determine what you enjoy the most, what you dislike, and what does not bring in dollars.

- If you spend 95 percent of your time on activities you don't like and that don't make you any money, increase the amount of time you spend on the activities that you like and that make you money.

- Hire someone to do the activities you do not like for about $15 an hour. Hire a courier service to pick up and deliver packages for about $10 or $12 a run. This saves me a couple of hours a day sitting in traffic and being stressed out. It also gives me more time to find good deals.

- Hire experienced managers to manage your property for 8 to 10 percent of rents collected. Then manage the managers, and make sure they do a good job.

- Get out of the contracting and repair business. Hire people to do it and manage them, or hire someone to manage them.

- Hire an administrative assistant or bring someone in as a quasi-partner to do bookkeeping, filing, phone answering, and so on. That will free you to make more money doing more deals.

Track Your Deals

It is important to understand and track what one deal is worth to you. If you find one property and wholesale it for $8,000, it probably only took 5 to 15 hours to do that. Again, every week, review how you spend your time and what makes you money, and spend more time on the things that make you money.

Have Fun with It

My goal (and your goal) is to have fun in real estate investing and make it profitable for years to come. That is why you want to develop a stellar reputation, to do what you say you will do when you do it. If you can't afford to do something, don't do it. If you put a contract in on a property, make sure you have enough information so you can close on it and not let others down. If you are not conscientious, you will gain a bad reputation and no one will want to do business with you.

For example, if you are wholesaling properties, make sure that you leave others who are involved enough room to make a good profit. If they make as much as or more than you, they will keep coming back. If you do not let them profit, they will be gone. Remember, two or three good clients can make you hundreds of thousands of dollars a year, every year, for dozens of years.

CHAPTER 12

Somewhere, something incredible is waiting to be known.
—CARL SAGAN

Your Action Plan

From reading this book, you have a lot of information about how to find deals, how to analyze them, how to contract them, how to wholesale them, how to lease-option them, how to hold them, and how to buy them, fix them up, and sell them. Now what do you do?

Make your own action plan. Decide where you want to be in the next 30, 60, and 90 days. What will you have achieved in 1 year? In 5 years? 10? 20? Most important, what activities will get you there?

Follow Your Successes

Follow these basic policies and procedures of real estate investing, and keep track of what makes you money. Then do *more* of whatever that is! Whatever you did to find that one deal, do more of it. Whatever you enjoy doing, do it more often. Unfortunately, though, when something is working in life, most people decide to do something else. It is human nature.

Elements of Your Plan

The next 30 days are critical for getting you going in real estate investing. First, decide how you will earn your real estate income in the next 30 to 90 days or more. Will you earn it by flipping, lease-optioning, wholesaling, or buying, fixing up, and selling? Then set in motion these elements of your action plan that will lead you to success.

- *Belief.* Do you believe that you can be successful in real estate investing? If you are not sure, you know you can change your belief quickly. Start by closing your eyes and thinking, just for a minute, about why you are in real estate investing. What do you want to get out of it? What is your dream? What is your real goal? Keep your eyes closed, relax, breathe, see it, and imagine it. Tune in to what I call *a burning why*—why you are in business. To create more income for your family, achieve financial freedom, get more vacation time, walk away from a job or a boss, purchase your own home. What will real estate investing do for you? Six months or a year from now, if you ever feel frustrated, remember your burning why. That memory will keep you going.

- *Planning.* Every week, take 30 to 45 minutes to review your plan. Every six months, completely redo your plan, see where you were, where you are heading, and where you want to go next. The sky is the limit. Some of my students say, "I just want to handle commercial property and make hundreds of thousands of dollars a year wholesaling it." That is what they do. Some just want to own 12 properties in 10 years. Some people want to get 8 or 10 lease options going in nice neighborhoods, generating $2,000 to $4,000 of extra income per month. Always state a projected completion date, and set aside time every week to work on your goal, just like an exercise program. Hold that time sacred.

- *Being professional.* Imagine that you are talking with a motivated seller, and three different people, including yourself, are competing to buy a particular property. You pull out your professional real estate investor's portfolio because you want to show that you know what you are doing. You are acting in a professional way . . . and keep acting that way. Make sure *everyone knows* you are professional.

- *Motivation.* Spend time around people in your real estate association and those you have met through newspaper ads and at auctions. Have lunch with them, hear about their successes, and stay motivated. Why do millions of people go to church every Sunday? They go to reinforce what they are learning and to remind themselves about what they know, to renew their belief in themselves, to motivate themselves to live well, and to associate with others of similar beliefs.

- *Basic knowledge.* I hope you have that after reading this book. Put part of your income toward your education as well as toward making deals. People spend hundreds of thousands of dollars on law education, medicine, accounting, and engineering education to gain basic knowledge and keep up their qualifications. You are a professional, too; therefore, invest in your education. Go regularly to www.shemin.com to read continuously updated ideas and resources.

- *Take consistent action.* Make those phone calls. Look at properties. Most important, make offers. Whoever makes the most

Show Naysayers What You Can Do

If you have people in your life who try to steal your dreams by saying, "Real estate doesn't work," go out, flip a deal, hand over the check, and let them spend it. All of a sudden, they will become your biggest fans.

offers will probably get the most deals. Whoever looks at the most houses will probably get the most real estate. Whoever makes the most offers will probably make the most money. Write down your action plan and constantly remind yourself to keep networking, finding good deals, and making presentations to motivated sellers.

What Holds You Back?

You may still doubt that you can actually make it happen. When has doubt served you? Never. Doubt is like a little voice that keeps you from getting what you want. "I should have talked to that person. I should have made that phone call. I should have made that offer. I should have taken action." Doubt does not help you.

Having pride can also hold you back. That is when the little voice says, "I don't need that. I'm too good for that. Why would I do that? Who am I to drive around and look at a bunch of houses and write these silly offers?" You may have pride when you really need humility. When has pride served you? Never.

What is the antidote? Action. Look at a house. Make a phone call. Make an offer.

Become a professional real estate investor with various sources of income, and make your dreams come true.

Doubt is the beginning, not the end, of wisdom.
—GEORGE ILES

The Twenty-Five Costliest Mistakes That Almost Every Real Estate Investor Makes and How to Avoid Them

The costliest mistakes are listed, and then ways to avoid each of them are discussed.

1. You didn't get started in real estate investing soon enough.
2. You don't put every repair bid in writing.
3. You sell or rent property to people who cannot pay.
4. You don't have a plan.
5. You don't charge tenants for damage.
6. You don't screen your tenants, and then you have to evict them.
7. You pay for a repair or construction job before it is 100 percent complete.

8. You pay for a repair or remodeling, even though it is finished three weeks late.

9. You let your business run you: bookkeeping, tenants, potential buyers, and phone calls all keep you busy and stressed out.

10. You spend too much money on a house that you bought to fix up and sell.

11. You are running out of cash, and the bills keep coming.

12. You pay too much for repairs.

13. You analyze property too much: You look for one year and don't make any offers.

14. You spend too much time talking with tenants, worrying about repairs, doing paperwork, and making very little money.

15. You overlook bad houses in bad neighborhoods.

16. You don't have the proper insurance: Real estate is risky, and you may have legal problems and legal questions.

17. Your cash flow from your rental properties is not high enough.

18. You punish bad tenants, but you don't reward good ones.

19. You hate being a landlord because the tenants always bother you with their problems.

20. You hate collecting rent, or many of your tenants do not pay the rent.

21. You only look at your properties when there is a problem.

22. You miss out on special loan programs.

23. You find a good property, put it under contract, then find out that it is not a good deal; however, you are bound to close or be sued.

24. Your rehab house won't sell, or your rental house won't rent.

25. Your house will not sell fast enough, and you do not want to wait seven months to get your cash.

Bonus Points

26. You negotiated a good cash offer on a nice piece of property, but you left money on the table.

27. You have worked hard on your asset protection program, but it may not work because you used the term *asset protection*.

28. You do not have enough happy clients or tenants.

1. *You didn't get started in real estate investing soon enough.*

    Solution.   Get started! After having interviewed over 1,200 real estate investors, ranging in age from 18 to 86, it is amazing to find out that they all have one regret in common: "I wish I would have started sooner." Get the right information, read all the books you can, talk to other investors, and make offers. Conduct your first deal—it will be the most difficult one, but they get easier after that.

2. *You don't put every repair bid in writing.*

    Solution.   Put every repair bid in writing. Know exactly what will be done, what will be included, and what will not. Every material should be listed.

3. *You sell or rent property to people who cannot pay.*

    Solution.   Never sign a contract to sell or lease a property without knowing that the prospective buyer or renter is pre-approved. More than 50 percent of all real estate contracts fail because the buyers cannot get a new loan. Either talk with their mortgage banker or obtain from that banker a letter confirming that they are preapproved. *Preapproved* buyers have submitted their paperwork to the bank or mortgage company and are ready to close based on getting a contract, appraisal, and title work done.

    There is a big difference between preapproved and prequalified. *Prequalified* means that someone at the mortgage company or bank has told the buyers what they qualify for based on the buyers telling them what their income and debt are. However, the lending institution has not verified any of this information.

The same is true for renters. Screen them before you promise them a property, sign a lease, or take their deposit. This will help you by not tying up your properties with unqualified buyers or potential renters. I never sign a contract and tie up a property and my time until I am satisfied that the buyer is preapproved.

4. *You don't have a plan.*

   Solution. Every successful person and business has a plan! You need a long-term (1-, 5-, 10-, and 20-year) and a short-term plan (this week, this month, six-month). Set goals and track yourself. Whether you want to do 1 house or 1,000 houses, make a plan today!

5. *You don't charge tenants for damage.*

   Solution. Make sure that you state in your lease that tenants are responsible for damage(s) done by them or their guests. I give my tenants a list of common damages and what the charges are to repair them (e.g., a small hole in the wall: $60; broken window: $80). Unpaid damages become unpaid rent. If the rent is not paid, you should begin eviction. If you won't do it for yourself, do it for others. If you don't charge tenants for damages, they will think that they can break things and not be held responsible when they move into the next property.

6. *You don't screen your tenants, then you have to evict them.*

   Solution. Screen every potential renter by running both a credit and a criminal background check. Check with two previous landlords, and verify employment. Make the renters pay for these checks as part of their application fee.

7. *You pay for a repair or construction job before it is 100 percent complete.*

    Solution. Never pay for a job until it is 100 percent complete. If you do pay 100 percent before the job is done, there is little incentive for the contractor to finish. Give out as small a draw as possible. Avoid the temptation of thinking that the contractors have finished 96 percent of the job, it is Friday, and they want to be paid. One hundred percent is 100 percent. This is a business, run it like one.

8. *You pay for a repair or remodeling, even though it is finished three weeks late.*

    Solution. Time is money! If your house is not ready to show, sell, or rent because the contractor is late, then you are losing time and money. Always put a per-day late penalty in all of your contracts. (See the Procedures for Contractors in the appendix.) Be fair. Give your contractor an extra day or two, but then charge $25, $50, or $100 per day for every day that the job is not complete. Set your policies and procedures and enforce them.

9. *You let your business run you: bookkeeping, tenants, potential buyers, and phone calls all keep you busy and stressed out.*

    Solution. Set up a smart system to handle your calls, bookkeeping, renting, and selling processes. Run your business; don't let your business run you. Set policies and procedures, and follow them so you have no decisions to make. Real estate is a simple business. Run your business like all successful businesses. Set up policies and procedures, and stick to them. See the Formulating a Winning Strategy worksheet in the appendix for ways how to implement a worry-free system for success using very affordable technology and easy-to-use policies and procedures.

10. *You spend too much money on a house that you bought to fix up and sell.*

Solution. Don't overrehab your house! Know your market. The National Association of Realtors says that about 90 percent of buyers emotionally decide whether to buy within 1½ minutes of arriving at the curb. Therefore, you should spend your time and money on curb appeal and kitchens and bathrooms. Don't spend dollars unnecessarily. Look at new houses to find the "in" colors. Your rehab costs should only be about 75 percent of your net selling price. Don't forget to include carrying costs (e.g., interest, insurance, and paying yourself for your time). So many real estate investors say they made $10,000 on that house, but they forget to mention that they worked 20 hours a week on it for one year, thereby earning about $8 an hour.

11. *You are running out of cash, and the bills keep coming.*
    Solution. Put at least 15 percent of what you earn aside in something liquid (not alcohol). My banker once told me, "All that you real estate people have is real estate . . . get some cash or stocks." Always keep a cushion. If you sell something or earn some money, you need to escrow the money for taxes, insurance, and emergencies. Be conservative.

12. *You pay too much for repairs.*
    Solution. Break down every repair bid (whether it is for your house, car, computer, etc.) into (1) how much the materials cost and (2) how many labor hours it will take. For example, if a paint job is bid at $900, ask how much the paint will cost ($100), how many people and how long it will take to complete the job. If the answer is that the job will require two people for one day, that is $800 divided by 2 for an 8-hour day, and that's $50 an hour. It seems high for a painter. Break every bid down!

13. *You analyze property too much: You look for one year and don't make any offers.*

Solution. Stop paralysis of analysis. Practice real estate by the numbers. How much is the property worth? How much can I get it for? What are the repairs, carrying costs, and so on? Get the information. Make a decision and move on. Make offers—at least, make low ones. The person who makes the most money in real estate does it by making the most offers. That's the secret.

14. *You spend too much time talking with tenants, worrying about repairs, doing paperwork, and making very little money.*

Solution. Your time as a real estate investor is best spent looking for good deals. After you find a good deal, then you can keep it, flip it, lease-option it, or buy, fix, and sell it. You need to organize your business so you spend your time on what makes money for you. Keep track of your time, and study how you use it and what makes money for you. Stop doing the things that don't make money for you, or delegate them to others.

15. *You overlook bad houses in bad neighborhoods.*

Solution. Just because you don't like the house does not mean that you cannot make money with it. Other people live and buy in that area. Again, you need to learn how to flip and lease-option houses. Some of the best money in real estate is made in the bad neighborhoods with junky houses.

16. *You don't have the proper insurance: Real estate is risky, and you may have legal problems and legal questions.*

Solution. Be properly insured. Never ever buy a property without title insurance and good liability insurance. Make sure you have the right title, liability, and legal insurance. For just pennies a day, or $26 a month, for Pre-Paid Legal Services, Inc., you can sleep well at night knowing you have a top-rated law firm ready to defend you should you be sued and lawyers ready to answer any and all of your legal questions. Please don't invest in real estate without it. You can have a will prepared, have your contracts reviewed before you sign them, have letters written on your behalf to collect money owed to you or settle problems, be represented if you are sued, and have access to a tax attorney if you are audited—all for $26 a month. (See Chapter 10.)

17. *Your cash flow from your rental properties is not high enough.*
    Solution.   Raise the rent every year. So many landlords run their real estate businesses like a charity. Don't be afraid to raise rents. Your costs go up every year due to inflationary pressures. It doesn't have to be a large increase (in fact, mine are minor), but increase the rent! By raising rent in small increments each year, you will also avoid having to raise rent in large increments every three or so years. It's less painful for you and the tenants if you do it slowly. Your tenants may be angry, but when you remind them of the costs of moving, they will stop complaining . . . and stay . . . and pay. I always explain in a letter, toward the end of each lease, that it makes more sense to pay the small increase in rent rather than to pay new deposits, truck rental, switching utilities, and so on. If large increases are necessary, I usually provide something to the tenant to make the increase more palatable, such as carpet cleaning, a ceiling fan, and more.

18. *You punish bad tenants, but you don't reward good ones.*
    Solution.   Reward tenants every year. Although you might think I'm schizophrenic by telling you in item 17 to raise rents and then, here in item 18, to reward tenants for staying, you will see that it goes a long way toward making the tenants happy and toward increasing the value of your property. For instance, install a ceiling fan, a screen door, a brass doorknocker, or even clean the carpet as a reward for paying rent on time, being good tenants, or renewing their lease. Tell them

about the gift when they move in. Give them something to look forward to. When you give the gift to them, make it a big deal. Reward the good tenants, and get rid of the bad ones.

19. *You hate being a landlord because the tenants always bother you with their problems.*

Solution. The easiest way to get rid of those headaches is to put the tenants in charge of taking care of the property. How? Offer your tenants a lease-option agreement. Show them how home ownership will reduce their tax burden, even if they must pay more money per month to pay off the loan. Make sure that you have a separate lease and purchase agreement. If you don't, evicting the tenants could get nasty. Talk to an attorney in your state to make the proper moves. Remember, if you do a lease-option agreement, it is just as important to constantly inspect your investment (once a month is okay). Simply because the purchase aspect of the deal is supposed to reduce your headaches (and it does), it does not mean that the tenants will keep the place in proper order. Make sure, too, that the tenant is capable of making the repairs—many are not.

20. *You hate collecting rent, or many of your tenants do not pay the rent.*

Solution. Why not have the federal government pay your tenants' rents to you directly—every month—like clockwork? Familiarize yourself with the Section 8 Program, and find out how the government will ensure rent payments and insure you against tenant damages. I have become an expert in Section 8 housing and have found it to be incredibly easy (if you know what you are doing) and incredibly profitable! Also, the lease is guaranteed to a full year (in most places) once you pass the Section 8 officer's inspection. Section 8 is most appropriate for low- and moderate-income housing.

21. *You only look at your properties when there is a problem.*

Solution. Inspect your properties every 30 days. If you don't inspect your properties regularly, your tenants could give you a very ugly surprise. Thus, regular (and surprise) inspections will keep your tenants on their toes. Keep in mind that a $30,000 to $200,000 investment is nothing to sneeze at. Protect your investments—inspect them! Also, inspecting your properties will show that you care; you can be made aware of small problems and fix them before they become big ones.

22. *You miss out on special loan programs.*

Solution. Ask your local and state housing authorities and even local banks if they have special loan programs and how you can qualify for them. Also, many banks have Community Reinvestment Act (CRA) departments, which will provide you with better financing than you would typically find if you are operating in low- and moderate-income neighborhoods. Try to find sellers who would be willing to sell on owner's terms (where the owner is the lender) or by lease purchase (where your rental payments can be applied toward a down payment in the future).

Help the banks help you. If you are buying, rehabbing, and/or developing properties in low-income areas, remind the banks that they can get CRA credit. Many banks are under serious pressure from the federal government to make loans in the lower-income areas. Many banks aggressively seek out such loans. If you play your cards right, you can use this as leverage when negotiating with the banks.

23. *You find a good property, put it under contract, then find out that it is not a good deal; however, you are bound to close or be sued.*

Solution. Always put contingencies in your purchase agreements. Depending on how desperate your seller is, you may be able to get a whole host of contingencies in your purchase agreement. Why do you want contingencies? Contingencies provide you with an out. For example, suppose you find something wrong with the house between the time you sign the agreement and the closing date. You will be able to get out of the deal only if you've put in the proper contingency. Always try to put in a contingency so that you can walk away from any deal for almost any reason and at any time.

Typical contingency clauses include a home inspection, which gives you the right to reject the purchase agreement if you don't like the inspection report, as well as the purchase agreement is contingent upon your receiving favorable financing.

You always want a way out, just in case things don't work out or if you find a better deal. Also, make sure that your purchase agreement is binding. To make any contract binding, there must be *consideration,* or some sort of payment from the buyer to the seller. Make sure that at least $10 passes hands, and that it specifically notes this in the purchase agreement, to make it legal and binding. Ethically, *do not* put offers on properties that you do not realistically think you can close or flip.

24. *Your rehab house won't sell, or your rental house won't rent.*
    Solution. Increase the marketability of your investment. When selling your investment property, remember that the three most important areas are (1) the front of your house, (2) the kitchen(s), and (3) the bathroom(s). By taking the time and spending a little money, you can make your property easier to sell and actually receive a much better price. In the front yard, do some general landscaping (e.g., clean out the beds, weed), add some fresh paint, and perhaps shutters, a brass doorknocker, and even a nice mailbox. As for the kitchens and bathrooms, simply make sure that they are spotless. If you can make it look nicer by just spending a few dollars, go ahead and do it—the returns will be great. Brass kick plates, brass

entry lamps, ceiling fans, and flowers are all relatively inexpensive, and they can really help to make a property look great and sell or rent faster.

25. *Your house will not sell fast enough, and you do not want to wait seven months to get your cash.*

    Solution.   Auction your house instead of using a broker. Don't roll your eyes just yet! It has been shown that auctioning a house often brings a full market price and offers you the chance to sell it quickly (in fact, if you need to sell your investment property quickly, auctioning may be the best way to go). Most likely, you can close on a house sold at auction within two or three months after first contacting an auctioneer. Many houses can sit three, six, even more months on the market before the right buyer comes along. Then the buyer will typically need a minimum of 45 days to close.

    Auctions, if done correctly (good advertising and a good auctioneer), can be quick and profitable. You can set a minimum price to protect yourself (that is, make sure the minimum price is more than your mortgage amount). Keep in mind, also, that you have to pay for advertising and you have to pay the auctioneer an amount almost equal to what you would pay a commissioned real estate broker. Realize, however, that the advantage to an auction is speed; if you need out quickly, an auction may be the way to go.

26. *You negotiated a good cash offer on a nice piece of property, but you left money on the table.*

    Solution. Even if you are going to pay cash for a property, ask for owner's terms. If you get owner's terms, offer to pay cash, but get a discount. For example, find a house priced at $50,000 price; the owner's terms are $10,000 down, and you would need to obtain 20-year note for $40,000. Instead, offer cash at $46,000; you could save $4,000 that you might not have been able to save had you not asked for owner's terms.

27. *You have worked hard on your asset protection program, but it may not work because you used the term* asset protection.

    Solution. Never do anything solely for the purpose of asset protection. A really sharp attorney could drag you into court and prove that the only reason (your intent) to set up a trust or a partnership was for asset protection. This trust or partnership could then be undone if the attorney were to prove that this was your intent and that it was a *fraudulent conveyance.* Never use the words *asset protection,* and always document your reasons for creating trusts, partnerships, and corporations, such as for estate planning or tax purposes. Of course, be honest. Don't say or write anything that is not true.

28. *You do not have enough happy clients or tenants.*

    Solution. Give everyone more than they expect. You will convert them into long-term clients and long-term tenants. For example, I promised 25 problems/mistakes with solutions, and you have just read 3 bonus ones!

Tools for Running Your Real Estate Investment Business

T his appendix includes excellent tools to keep you organized and within legal guidelines for your real estate investing business. It includes forms and contract samples used by real estate investors to streamline their business. This selection of forms is not meant to be comprehensive, but rather a sampling of commonly used ones that have been developed and refined over the years. You'll find this extensive appendix is organized in three sections: (1) "Legal Forms," (2) "Sample Forms and Procedures," and (3) "Guidelines for Success."

If you would like to receive a full set of forms in a CD-ROM format, or if you would like to sign up for advanced seminars in real estate investing seminars, landlording, and asset protection, please call 888-302-8018, or visit www.shemin.com for full details.

List of Forms

The following list details the three categories of forms and contracts, as well as guidelines for success.

1. Legal Forms
   - Agreement for Deed
   - Agreement of Trust
   - Contract to Purchase Real Estate
   - Contract of Sale
   - Quit Claim Deed
   - Mortgage Purchase Agreement
   - Offer to Assign and Sell a Note and Deed of Trust
   - Land Installment Contract
   - Warranty Deed to Trustee
   - Promissory Note
   - Power of Attorney

2. Sample Forms and Procedures
   - Property Acquisition Worksheet
   - Hiring Contractors: Policy and Procedures
   - Rehab Worksheet
   - Procedures for Contractors
   - Loan Qualification Worksheet
   - Information Sheet for Notes (Loans)
   - Lease-Option Prospect Qualification Form
   - Letter to Potential Investors to Sell a Property
   - Letter to Insurer to Put Owner's Name on Policy

3. Guidelines for Success

- Guidelines for Successful Negotiating
- Negotiating Keys
- Property Business Plan Example: Greenwood Court Project
- Formulating a Winning Strategy

Appendix: Legal Forms

AGREEMENT FOR DEED

THIS AGREEMENT FOR DEED made this _____ day of A.D., 20____, BY AND BETWEEN _____ of the County of _____, State of _____, hereinafter referred to as SELLER, and _____ hereinafter referred to as PURCHASER.

WITNESSETH, that provided the said purchasers shall first make the payments and perform the covenants hereinafter set forth on their part to be made and performed, the said sellers covenant and agree to and will by good and sufficient warranty deed, convey, and assure to the said purchasers, their heirs, and assigns forever in fee simple, free, and clear of all encumbrances, the following described land situated in _____ County, _____ to wit:

The purchase price of said land is $_____, of which the purchasers have herewith paid to the sellers the sum of $_____, and the purchasers agree to pay to the sellers the balance, to wit: the principal sum of _____ dollars, together with interest on so much of said principal sum as remains from time to time outstanding and unpaid at the rate of per centrum from _____ until paid; said principal and interest to be payable in payments consecutive on the _____ day of each and every month beginning with the _____ day of _____, 20____; said installments to be applied first to interest and balance to principal. If any payment is not received within _____ days of due date, there shall be a late charge of _____% added. The purchasers may prepay any part of the principal sum hereof in multiples of $_____ on any installment payment date, but any such prepayment shall not relieve the purchasers from making the payment of the installment then due and any subsequent installment provided hereby unless at the time of such prepayment the purchasers pay all sums unpaid hereon.

The PURCHASERS covenant and agree as follows: (a) to pay all taxes, fines, and assessments levied or assessed on said land subsequent to December 31, 20____, as and when the same respectively become due and shall exhibit to sellers immediately after such payment the official receipts therefore; (b) to place and continuously keep on the building now or hereafter situated on said land fire and extended-coverage insurance in the usual standard policy form in a sum not less than $_____ in such company or companies as may be approved by the sellers, and said policies shall be delivered up and held by the sellers and contain the usual clauses making said policies payable to the sellers as their interest may appear, and in the event any sum of money becomes payable under such policies, the sellers shall have the right to receive and apply the sum on account of the indebtedness secured hereby; (c) to permit, commit, or suffer no waste, impairment, or deterioration of said property or any part thereof; (d) to at all times keep and maintain the buildings and improvements on said land in a good and tenantable state of repair and condition.

Time is of the essence in this agreement, and in the event of any breach of this agreement or default on the part of the purchasers of any kind whatsoever, the sellers may without notice to the purchasers exercise the following options: (a) to terminate this agreement and retain all sums of money theretofore paid by the purchasers as liquidated damages and/or the reasonable rental value of said land, and to render said premises and take possession thereof fully and to all intents and purposes as if the purchasers had no interest in said property whatsoever, or (b) to accelerate all sums of money secured by this agreement whether due by the literal terms hereof or not, and to foreclose this agreement in accordance with the rules of practice applicable to vendors' liens, in which event the purchasers agree to pay all costs of collection and foreclosure, including a reasonable attorney's fee.

The words *seller, sellers, purchaser,* and *purchasers,* whether in the singular or plural as the case may be wherever used herein, shall be taken to mean and include the singular, if only one, and plural, jointly and severally, if more than one, and their respective heirs, assigns, and legal representatives; and, that the word *their* taken to mean his, her, or its wherever the context hereof so implies or admits.

IN WITNESS WHEREOF, the parties hereto have hereunto set their hands and seals the day and year first above written.

_____	_____
Witness	SELLER
_____	
Witness	
_____	_____
Witness	PURCHASER
_____	
Witness	

STATE OF: _____
COUNTY OF: _____

Before me personally appeared _____ to me well known and known to me to be the person(s) described in and who executed the foregoing instrument, and acknowledged to and before me that he executed said instrument for the purpose therein expressed.

WITNESS my hand seal, and official seal this ____ day of _____, 20____.

Notary Public: _____
State of: _____
My Commission Expires: _____

STATE OF:_____

COUNTY OF: _____

Before me personally appeared _____ to me well known and known to me to be the person(s) described in and who executed the foregoing instrument, and acknowledged to and before me that he executed said instrument for the purpose therein expressed.

WITNESS my hand seal, and official seal this ____ day of _____, 20____.

Notary Public: _____
State of: _____
My Commission Expires: _____

This instrument was prepared by: _____

AGREEMENT OF TRUST

THIS AGREEMENT AND DECLARATION OF TRUST is made and entered into this _____ day of _____, 20____, by and between _____, as Grantors and Beneficiary (hereinafter referred to as the *Beneficiary* or *Beneficiaries*, whether one or more, which designation shall include all successors in interest of any beneficiary), and _____ whose address is _____ (hereinafter referred to as the *Trustee*, which designation shall include all successor trustees).

IT IS MUTUALLY AGREED AS FOLLOWS:

1. *Trust Property.* The Beneficiary is about to convey or cause to be conveyed to the Trustee by deed, absolute in form, the property described in the attached *Exhibit A*, which said property shall be held by the Trustee, in trust, for the following uses and purposes, under the terms of this Agreement and shall be hereinafter referred to as the *Trust Property*.
2. *Consideration.* No consideration has been paid by Trustee for such conveyance. The conveyance will be accepted and will be held by Trustee subject to all existing encumbrances, easements, restrictions, or other clouds or claims against the title thereto, whether the same are of record or otherwise. The property will be held on the trusts, terms, and conditions and for the purposes hereinafter set forth, until the whole of the trust estate is conveyed, free of this trust, as hereinafter provided.
3. *Beneficiary.* The person(s) named in the attached *Exhibit B* are the Beneficiary(ies) of this Trust (referred to as *Beneficiary* or *Beneficiaries*), and as such, shall be entitled to all of the earnings, avails, and proceeds of the Trust Property according to their interests set opposite their respective names.
4. *Interests.* The interests of the Beneficiary shall consist solely of the following rights respecting the Trust Property:

a. The right to direct the Trustee to convey or otherwise deal with the title to the Trust Property as hereinafter set out.
b. The right to manage and control the Trust Property.
c. The right to receive the proceeds and avails from the rental, sale, mortgage, or other disposition of the Trust Property.

The foregoing rights shall be deemed to be personal property and may be assigned and otherwise transferred as such. No beneficiary shall have any legal or equitable right, title, or interest as realty, in or to any real estate held in trust under this Agreement, or the right to require partition of that real estate, but shall have only the rights, as personally set out above, and the death of a beneficiary shall not terminate this Trust or in any manner affect the powers of the Trustee.

1. *Power of Trustee.*
   a. With the consent of the Beneficiary, the Trustee shall have authority to issue notes or bonds and to secure the payment of the same by mortgaging the whole or any part of the Trust Property; to borrow money, giving notes therefore signed by him in his capacity as Trustee; to invest such part of the capital and the profits there from and the proceeds of the sale of bonds and notes in such real estate, equities in real estate, and mortgages in real estate in the United States of America, as he may deem advisable.
   b. With the consent of the Beneficiary, the Trustee shall have the authority to hold the legal title to all of the Trust Property, and shall have the exclusive management and control of the property as if he were the absolute owner thereof, and the Trustee is hereby given full power to do all things and perform all acts which in his judgment are necessary and proper for the protection of the Trust Property and for the interest of the Beneficiary in the property of the Trust, subject to the restrictions, terms, and conditions herein set forth.

c. Without prejudice to the general powers conferred on the Trustee hereunder, it is hereby declared that the Trustee shall have the following powers, with the consent of the Beneficiary:

(1) To purchase any real property for the Trust at such times and on such terms as may seem advisable; to assume mortgages upon the property.

(2) To sell at public auction or private sale, to barter, to exchange, or to otherwise dispose of any part, or the whole of the Trust Property which may from time to time form part of the Trust estate, subject to such restrictions and for such consideration for cash and/or for credit, and generally upon such terms and conditions as may seem judicious, to secure payment upon any loan or loans of the Trust, by mortgage with or without power of sale, and to include such provisions, terms, and conditions as may seem desirable.

(3) To rent or lease the whole or any part of the Trust Property for long or short terms, but not for terms exceeding the term of the Trust then remaining.

(4) To repair, alter, tear down, add to, or erect any building or buildings upon land belonging to the Trust; to fill, grade, drain, improve, and otherwise develop any land belonging to the Trust; to carry on, operate, or manage any building, apartment house, or hotel belonging to the Trust.

d. To make, execute, acknowledge, and deliver all deeds, releases, mortgages, leases, contracts, agreements, instruments, and other obligations of whatsoever nature relating to the Trust Property, and generally to have full power to do all things and perform all acts necessary to make the instruments proper and legal.

e. To collect notes, obligations, dividends, and all other payments that may be due and payable to the Trust; to deposit the proceeds thereof, as well as any other monies from whatsoever source they may be derived, in any suitable bank or depository, and to draw the same from time to time for the purposes herein provided.

f. To pay all lawful taxes and assessments and the necessary expenses of the Trust; to employ such of officers, brokers, engineers, architects, carpenters, contractors, agents, counsel, and such other persons as may seem expedient, to designate their duties and fix their compensation; to fix a reasonable compensation for their own services to the Trust, as organizers thereof.

g. To represent the Trust and the Beneficiary in all suits and legal proceedings relating to the Trust Property in any court of law of equity, or before any other bodies or tribunals; to begin suits and to prosecute them to final judgment or decree; to compromise claims or suits, and to submit the same to arbitration when, in their judgment, such course is necessary or proper.

h. To arrange, pay for, and keep in force in the name and for the benefit of the Trustee, such insurance as the Trustee may deem advisable, in such companies, in such amounts, and against such risks as determined necessary by the Trustee.

2. *Duties of Trustee.* It shall be the duty of the Trustee, in addition to the other duties herein imposed upon him:

a. To keep a careful and complete record of all the beneficial interests in the Trust Property with the name and residence of the person or persons owning such beneficial interest, and such other items as they may deem of importance or as may be required by the Beneficiary.

b. To keep careful and accurate books showing the receipts and disbursements of the Trust and also of the Trust Property, and such other items as he may deem of importance or as the Beneficiary hereunder may require.

c. To keep books of the Trust open to the inspection of the Beneficiary at such reasonable times at the main office of the Trust as they may appoint.

d. To furnish the Beneficiary at special meetings, at which the same shall be requested, a careful, accurate, written report of their transactions as Trustees hereunder, of the financial standing of the Trust, and of such other information concerning the affairs of the Trust as they shall request.

e. To sell the Trust Property and distribute the proceeds there from:

(1) If any property shall remain in trust under this Agreement for a term which exceeds that allowed under applicable state law, the Trustee forthwith shall sell same at public sale after a reasonable public advertisement and reasonable notice to the Beneficiary and, after deducting its reasonable fees and expenses, the Trustee shall divide the proceeds of the sale among the then Beneficiaries as their interests may then appear, without any direction or consent whatsoever, or

(2) To transfer, set over, convey, and deliver to all the then Beneficiaries of this Trust their respective, undivided interests in any nondivisible assets, or

(3) To transfer, set over, and deliver all of the assets of the Trust to its then Beneficiaries, in their respective proportionate shares, at any time when the assets of the Trust consist solely of cash.

3. *Compensation of Trustee.* The Beneficiary jointly and severally agrees that the Trustee shall receive reasonable compensation monthly for his services as Trustee hereunder.

a. *Liability of Trustee.* The Trustee and his successor as Trustee shall not be required to give a bond, and each Trustee shall be liable only for his own acts and then only as a result of his own gross negligence or bad faith.

b. *Removal of Trustee.* The Beneficiary shall have the power to remove a Trustee from his office or appoint a successor to succeed him.

c. *Resignation and Successor.*

(1) Any Trustee may resign his office with thirty (30) days' written notice to Beneficiary, and Beneficiary

shall proceed to elect a new Trustee to take the place of the Trustee who had resigned, but the resignation shall not take effect until a certificate thereof, signed, sealed, and acknowledged by the new Trustee and a certificate of the election of the new Trustee, signed and sworn to by the Beneficiary and containing an acceptance of the office, signed and acknowledged by the new Trustee, shall have been procured in a form which is acceptable for recording in the registries of deeds of all the counties in which properties held under this instrument are situated. If the Beneficiary shall fail to elect a new Trustee within thirty (30) days after the resignation, then the Trustee may petition any appropriate court in this state to accept his resignation and appoint a new Trustee.

(2) Any vacancy in the office of Trustee, whether arising from death or from any other cause not herein provided for, shall be filled within thirty (30) days from the date of the vacancy, and the Beneficiary shall proceed to elect a new Trustee to fill the vacancy, and immediately thereafter shall cause to be prepared a certificate of the election containing an acceptance of the office, signed, sealed, and acknowledged by the new Trustee, which shall be in a form acceptable for recording in the registries of deeds of all the counties in which properties held under this instrument are situated.

(3) Whenever a new Trustee shall have been elected or appointed to the office of Trustee and shall have assumed the duties of office, he shall succeed to the title of all the properties of the Trust and shall have all the powers and be subject to all the restrictions granted to or imposed upon the Trustee by this agreement, and every Trustee shall have the powers, rights, and interests regarding the Trust Property, and shall be subject to the same restrictions and duties as the

original Trustee, except as the same shall have been modified by amendment, as herein provided for.

(4) Notwithstanding any such resignation, the Trustee shall continue to have a lien on the Trust Property for all costs, expenses, and attorney's fees incurred and for said Trustee's reasonable compensation.

4. *Objects and Purposes of Trust.* The objects and purposes of this Trust shall be to hold title to the Trust Property and to protect and conserve it until its sale or other disposition or liquidation. The Trustee shall not undertake any activity not strictly necessary to the attainment of the foregoing objects and purposes, nor shall the Trustee transact business within the meaning of applicable state law, or any other law, nor shall this Agreement be deemed to be, or create or evidence the existence of a corporation, de facto or de jure, or a Massachusetts Trust, or any other type of business trust, or an association in the nature of a corporation, or a partnership or joint venture by or between the Trustee and the Beneficiary, or by or between the Beneficiary.

a. *Exculpation.* The Trustee shall have no power to bind the Beneficiary personally and, in every written contract he may enter into, reference shall be made to this declaration; and any person or corporation contracting with, the Trustee, as well as any beneficiary, shall look to the funds and the Trust Property for payment under such contract, or for the payment of any debt, mortgage, judgment, or decree, or for any money that may otherwise become due or payable, whether by reason or failure of the Trustee to perform the contract, or for any other reason, and neither the Trustee nor the Beneficiary shall be liable personally therefore.

b. *Dealings with Trustee.* No party dealing with the Trustee in relation to the Trust Property in any manner whatsoever, and, without limiting the foregoing, no party to whom the property or any part of it or any interest in it shall be conveyed, contracted to be sold, leased, or mortgaged by the Trustee, shall be obliged to see to the application of any purchase money, rent, or money borrowed or otherwise advanced on the property; to see that the terms of this Trust Agreement have been complied with; to inquire into the authority, necessity, or expediency of any act of the Trustee, or be privileged to inquire into any of the terms of this Trust Agreement. Every deed, mortgage, lease, or other instrument executed by the Trustee in relation to the Trust Property shall be conclusive evidence in favor of every person claiming any right, title, or interest under the Trust that at the time of its delivery, the Trust created under this Agreement was in full force and effect; and that instrument was executed in accordance with the terms and conditions of this agreement and all its amendments, if any, and is binding upon all Beneficiaries under it; that the Trustee was duly authorized and empowered to execute and deliver every such instrument; if a conveyance has been made to a successor or successors in trust, that the successor or successors have been appointed properly and are vested fully with all the title, estate, rights, powers, duties, and obligations of its, his, or their predecessor in Trust.

c. *Recording of Agreement.* This Agreement shall not be placed on record in the county in which the Trust Property is situated, or elsewhere, but if it is so recorded, that recording shall not be considered as notice of the rights of any person under this Agreement derogatory to the title of powers of the Trustee.

d. *Name of Trustee.* The name of the Trustee shall not be used by the Beneficiary in connection with any advertising or other publicity whatsoever without the written consent of the Trustee.

e. *Income Tax Returns.* The Trustee shall be obligated to file any income tax returns with respect to the Trust, as required by law, and the Beneficiaries individually shall report and pay their share of income taxes on the earnings and avails of the Trust Property or growing out of their interest under this Trust.

f. *Assignment.* The interest of a Beneficiary, of any part of that interest, may be transferred only by a written assignment executed in duplicate and delivered to the Trustee. The Trustee shall note his acceptance on the original and duplicate original of the assignment retaining the original and delivering the duplicate original to the assignee as and for his or her evidence of ownership of a beneficial interest under this Agreement. No assignment of any interest under this Agreement, other than by operation of law, that is not so executed, delivered, and accepted shall be valid without the written approval of all of the other Beneficiaries, if any, who possess the power of direction. No person who is vested with the power of direction, but who is not a Beneficiary under this Agreement, shall assign that power without the written consent of all of the Beneficiaries.

g. *Individual Liability of Trustee.* The Trustee shall not be required, in dealing with the Trust Property or in otherwise acting under this Agreement, to enter into any individual contract or other individual obligation whatsoever; nor to make himself individually liable to pay or incur the payment of any damages, attorneys' fees, fines, penalties, forfeitures, costs, charges, or other sums of money whatsoever. The Trustee shall have no individual liability or obligation whatsoever arising from its ownership, as Trustee, of the legal title to the Trust Property, or with respect to any act done or contract entered into or indebtedness incurred by him in dealing with the Trust Property or in otherwise acting under this Agreement, except only as far as the Trust Property and any trust funds in the actual possession of the Trustee shall be applicable to the payment and discharge of that liability or obligation.

h. *Reimbursement and Indemnification of Trustee.* If the Trustee shall pay or incur any liability to pay any money on account of this Trust, or incur any liability to pay any money on account of being made a party to any litigation as a result of holding title to the Trust Property or otherwise in connection with this Trust, whether because of breach of contract, injury to person or property, fines or penalties under any law, or otherwise, the Beneficiaries, jointly and severally agree that on demand they will pay to the Trustee, with interest at the maximum rate allowed under the laws of the State of Tennessee per annum, all such payments made or liabilities incurred by the Trustee, together with its expenses, including reasonable attorneys' fees, and that they will indemnity and hold the Trustee harmless of and from any and all payments made or liabilities incurred by him for any reason whatsoever as a result of this Agreement; and all amounts so paid by the Trustee, as well as his compensation under this Agreement, shall constitute a lien on the Trust Property. The Trustee shall not be required to convey or otherwise deal with Trust Property as long as any money is due to the Trustee under this Agreement; nor shall the Trustee be required to advance or pay out any money on account of this Trust or to prosecute or defend any legal proceedings involving this Trust or any property or interest under this Agreement unless he shall be furnished with sufficient funds or be indemnified to his satisfaction.

(1) *Entire Agreement.* This Agreement contains the entire understanding between the parties and may be amended, revoked, or terminated only by written agreement signed by the Trustee and all of the Beneficiaries.

(2) *Governing Law.* This Agreement, and all transactions contemplated hereby, shall be governed by, construed, and enforced in accordance with the laws of the State of _____ applicable to contracts executed and performed in _____. The parties waive any right to a trial by jury and agree to submit to the

personal jurisdiction and venue of a court of subject matter jurisdiction location in _____ County, State of _____. In the event that litigation results from or arises out of the agreement or the performance thereof, the parties agree to reimburse the prevailing party's reasonable attorney's fees, court costs, and all other expenses, whether or not taxable by the court as costs, in addition to any other relief to which the prevailing party may be entitled. In such event, no action shall be entertained by said court or any court of competent jurisdiction if filed more than one year subsequent to the date the cause(s) of action actually accrued regardless of whether damages were otherwise, as of said time, calculable.

(3) *Binding Effect.* The terms and conditions of this agreement shall inure to the benefit of and be binding upon any successor trustee under it, as well as upon the executors, administrators, heirs, assigns, and all other successors-interest of the Beneficiaries.

(4) *Trustee's Liability to Beneficiaries.* The Trustee shall be liable to the Beneficiaries for the value of their respective beneficial interests only to the extent of the property held in trust by him hereunder, and the Beneficiaries shall enforce such liability only against the trust property and not against the Trustee personally.

(5) *Annual Statements.* There shall be no annual meeting of the Beneficiaries, but the Trustee shall prepare an annual report of their receipts and disbursements for the preceding fiscal year, which fiscal year shall coincide with the calendar year, and a copy of the report shall be sent by mail to the Beneficiaries not later than February 28 of each year.

(6) *Termination.* This trust may terminate at any time by a majority of the Beneficiaries and within thirty (30) days' written notice of termination delivered to the Trustee, the Trustee shall execute any and all doc-

uments necessary to vest fee simple marketable title to any and all trust property in the Beneficiary.

In Witness Whereof, the parties hereto have executed this agreement as of the day and year first above written.

Beneficiary:

_____

_____

Trustee

STATE OF: _____

COUNTY OF: _____

Personally appeared before me, _____, a Notary Public in and for the State and County aforesaid, _____, the within named bargainer, with whom I am personally acquainted (or proved to me on the basis of satisfactory evidence), and who acknowledged that he executed the foregoing instrument for the purposes therein contained.

WITNESS my hand and seal at office, on this ____ day of _____, 20____.
Notary Public: _____
State of: _____
My Commission Expires: _____

STATE OF: _____

COUNTY OF: _____

Personally appeared before me, _____, a Notary Public in and for the State and County aforesaid, _____, the within-named bargainer, with whom I am personally acquainted (or proved to me on the basis of satisfactory evidence), and who acknowledged that he executed the foregoing instrument for the purposes therein contained.

WITNESS my hand and seal at office, on this ____ day of
_____, 20____.
Notary Public: _____
State of: _____
My Commission Expires: _____

EXHIBIT A
Legal Description

EXHIBIT B
Beneficiaries and Their Interests
Name and Address   *% of Interest*

_____   _____

_____   _____

100%

CONTRACT TO PURCHASE REAL ESTATE

I/We offer to purchase from Seller the following described real estate, together with all improvements thereon and all appurtenant rights, located at:

Address: _____ City: _____

County: _____ State: _____ Zip: _____

The purchase price is to be $_____ payable as follows:

The conditions of the Purchase are as follows:

Subject to review, inspection, and written approval of my financial partner.

Purchaser shall have the right to assign his/her interest in this contract prior to escrow. Seller agrees to allow purchaser to show property to prospective partners and clients prior to closing.

Is there an Addendum to this contract? Yes _____ No _____

Is this deal "All Cash" or "Terms"? "All Cash" _____ "Terms" _____

Possession is to be given on or before _____.

Seller agrees to pay all Taxes and Assessments up to and including the month of _____, 20____.

Closing costs shall be paid by: Seller _____ Purchaser _____ Split ___

Closing date shall be on or before _____, 20____, with title to the previously described real estate to be conveyed by Warranty Deed with release of dower. Title is to be free, clear, and unencumbered, free of building orders, subject to zoning regulations of record, and except easements and restrictions of record.

This offer, when accepted, comprises the entire agreement of Purchaser and Seller, and it is agreed that no other representation or agreements have been made or relied upon.

This offer is to remain open for acceptance until _____.

Date: _____   Date: _____
Seller: _____   Purchaser: _____
Seller: _____   Purchaser: _____

CONTRACT OF SALE

THIS CONTRACT of sale made this _____ day of _____ 20____, by and between _____, hereinafter called SELLER, and _____, hereinafter called BUYER.

WITNESSETH: That the seller in considerations of the sum of _____ Dollars as earnest money and in part payment of the purchase price has this day sold and does hereby agree to convey by a good and valid warranty deed to said buyer, or to such person as he may in writing direct the following described real estate in _____ County, in the state of _____, to wit:

CONSIDERATION: Buyer agrees to purchase said real estate and to pay therefore the sum of _____ Dollars, upon the following terms: $_____ cash, balance.

MISCELLANEOUS CONDITIONS:

TITLE INSURANCE: The _____ or his agent, at seller's expense, agrees to make application to the _____ for Title Insurance on the aforementioned property, and if after examination by this Company the title is found insurable, the buyer hereby agrees to accept a title Policy issued by said Company in its usual form and to comply with this contract. WITHIN 10 DAYS after receiving a report on the title, and it is agreed that such report shall be conclusive evidence of good title subject to the exceptions therein stated, otherwise that the earnest money is to be refunded.

Should the buyer default in the performance of this contract on his part at the time and in the manner specified, then at seller's option the earnest money shall be forfeited as liquidated damages. But such forfeiture shall not prevent suit for the specific performance of this contract.

In the event of default in the terms of this contract for any reason on the part of the seller and in the event it becomes necessary, due to any fault of the sellers that the earnest money herein shown previously, must be returned to the buyer, then the seller shall be liable to the agent herein for the full commission set out in this contract.

The words SELLER and BUYER when used in this contract shall be construed as plural whenever the number of parties to this contract so requires.

SELLER ACKNOWLEDGMENT: Seller acknowledges that buyer is a licensed Real Estate Broker and is purchasing said property for rental or resale.

ADJUSTMENTS TO BE MADE AT TIME OF CLOSING:

(1) Seller's Escrow Deposits to be _____

(2) Taxes for Current Year _____

(3) Seller's Fire Insurance to be _____

(4) Existing Leases or Rents _____

Possession to be _____

Conveyance to be subject to existing Building Restrictions and/or Zoning Ordinances _____. Seller to bear risk of hazard loss to date of deed.

Purchaser: _____
Seller: _____

Purchaser: _____
Seller: _____

Deed Property to: _____

QUIT CLAIM DEED

ADDRESS New Owners: Name Street Address or Route Number City, State, Zip	SEND TAX BILLS to: Name Street Address or Route Number City, State, Zip	MAP PARCEL number:

FOR AND IN CONSIDERATION of One Dollar ($1.00), cash in hand paid, the receipt of which is hereby acknowledged, I _____, by these presents do hereby quit claim and convey unto _____ successors and assigns, all _____ rights, title and interest in and to the following, described tract of land:

STATE OF: _____
COUNTY OF: _____

The actual consideration for this transfer is $_____. Subscribed and sworn to before me this the ____ day of _____, 20____.

Notary Public: _____
State of: _____
My commission expires: _____
        (Affix Seal)

Said property is conveyed subject to such limitations, restrictions, and encumbrances as may affect the premises.

Witness _____ hand _____ this ____ day of _____, 20____, the corporate party, if any, having caused its name to be signed hereto by its duly authorized officers on said day and date.

_____   _____

MORTGAGE PURCHASE AGREEMENT

This agreement is made and entered into this _____ day of _____, 20____, by and between _____ located at _____, hereinafter referred to as the SELLER and _____, located at _____, hereinafter referred to as the BUYER.

WHEREAS, SELLER holds and owns a certain note in the face amount of $_____ bearing interest at the rate of ____ percent per annum with a remaining unpaid principal balance on the date hereof of approximately $_____, I secured by a mortgage or trust deed on certain real estate within the County of _____, State of _____, the street address of which property is:

_____

_____

_____

known as the MORTGAGE, a copy of the note and mortgage are attached hereto.

NOW, THEREFORE, SELLER and BUYER do hereby agree as follows:

1. SELLER agrees to sell _____ payments at a/an payment amount of $_____ and a balloon payment, if applicable, of $_____, due _____ for $_____ to the BUYER or any purchaser(s) secured by BUYER.

2. SELLER warrants that the representations with respect to the MORTGAGE are correct on the date hereof, that prompt notice to BUYER will be given of any default in the MORT-GAGE, and that title to the property serving as security for repayment of the note is marketable except for the lien created by the MORTGAGE and any senior mortgages or deeds of trust to wit:

FURTHER, SELLER warrants that the property serving as security for repayment of the note will appraise, by an independent appraiser selected by BUYER, at a value acceptable to Buyer. Should the property serving as security for the repayment of the note not appraise at this value or higher, SELLER agrees to reimburse BUYER for the appraisal fee plus any other documented out-of-pocket expenses, and this agreement shall terminate.

3. Should SELLER refuse to consummate the closing of this said sale, then SELLER agrees to reimburse BUYER for all documented out-of-pocket expenses including, but not limited to, appraisals, title searches, and credit checks. A $100.00 administration fee will also be due.

4. In the event the documents reflect information different than that represented by SELLER, the payor's creditworthiness is found to be unsatisfactory, title defects are of record, or other circumstances reflect unfavorably on the purchase, BUYER may terminate this agreement.

5. BUYER represents that BUYER does, from time to time but without obligation to do so, purchase mortgages and deeds of trust for his own account. SELLER acknowledges receipt of this disclosure that BUYER may purchase the mortgage, for his own account, to hold or resell. SELLER agrees that any purchase and subsequent resale of the MORTGAGE shall not in any way constitute a breach of any fiduciary duty owed by BUYER to SELLER.

6. A facsimile of this document shall be deemed and considered as an original, binding, and enforceable document.

Dated as listed previously.

Seller: _____

Seller: _____

Buyer: _____

OFFER TO ASSIGN AND SELL A NOTE AND DEED OF TRUST

FOR VALUABLE CONSIDERATION, I (we), the undersigned _____ (SELLER), offer and agree to assign, convey, and sell to (BUYER), his successors, or assigns, the note and deed of trust held by the undersigned on which the PAYOR is: (Name, address, and phone of Payor) for _____ DOLLARS to be paid as follows: (Terms and schedule of purchase payment)

The said deed of trust is recorded in _____ County, State of _____, in the Registry of Deeds, BOOK ____, PAGE ____, and dated _____.

Property address is _____.

The approximate principal balance as of _____ on said note and deed of trust is $_____, and the monthly payment is $_____ per month. There are _____ payments remaining. Next payment is due on _____.

The PAYOR has been late in making payments, and the payments are now _____ months in arrears.

I (we) fully warrant that I have disclosed all information of which a prudent purchaser should be aware.

The BUYER, his successors, or assigns shall have until _____ to exercise and accept this offer to assign and sell. Acceptance shall be by written notice to the seller, with the settlement to be held on or before at _____.

At settlement, seller will provide, in addition to the ORIGINAL NOTE and the ORIGINAL DEED OF TRUST, the following:

Seller is advised that this is a binding contract to assign and to sell the preceding described note and deed of trust, and if it is not fully understood, legal counsel should be consulted before signing.

Dated: _____

_____   _____
ASSIGNOR   ASSIGNOR

LAND INSTALLMENT CONTRACT

THIS AGREEMENT is made and entered into by and between _____, hereinafter called the *Vendor,* and _____, hereinafter called the *Vendee.*

WITNESSETH: The Vendor, for himself, his heirs, and assigns, does hereby agree to sell to the Vendee, his heirs, and assigns the following described real estate together with all appurtenances, rights, privileges, and easements, and all buildings and fixtures in their present condition located upon said property.

1. Contract Price, Method of Payment, Interest Rate

In consideration whereof, the Vendee agrees to purchase the aforementioned property for the sum of _____ Dollars ($_____), payable as follows:

The sum of $_____ as down payment at the time of execution of the within Land Installment Contract, the receipt of which is hereby acknowledged, leaving a principal balance owed by Vendee of $_____, together with interest on the unpaid balance payable in consecutive monthly installments of $_____, beginning on the ____ day of _____, 20____, and on the ____ day of each and every month thereafter until said balance and interest are paid in full, or until the ____ day of whichever event occurs first. The interest on the unpaid balance due hereon shall be ____ (%) percent per annum computed monthly, in accordance with a _____-month amortization schedule during the life of this Contract.

Payments shall be credited first to the interest, and the remainder to the principal or other sums due Vendor. The total amount of this obligation, both principal and interest, unpaid after making any such Application of payments as herein receipted, shall be the interest-bearing principal amount of this obligation for the next succeeding interest computation period. If any payment is not received within ____ days of payment date, there shall be a late charge of (____%) percent assessed. The Vendee may pay the entire purchase price on this contract without prepayment penalty. The monthly installments shall be payable as directed by the Vendor herein.

2. Encumbrances

Said real estate is presently subject to a mortgage, and the Vendor shall not place any additional mortgage on the premises without the first written permission of the Vendee. In the event the Vendor should become delinquent in payments on the mortgage, the Vendee may pay the same and credit said payment to the contract price.

3. Evidence of Title

The Vendor shall be required to provide an abstract or guarantee of title, statement of title, title insurance, or such other evidence of title.

4. Recording of Contract

The Vendor shall cause a copy of this contract to be recorded in the _____ County Recorder's Office within a period of twenty (20) days after the execution of this Contract by the parties hereto.

5. Real Estate Taxes

Real estate taxes shall be prorated to the date of the closing using the short-term method of tax proration being those becoming due and payable on _____, 20____. When the real estate taxes become due and payable, the Vendee shall pay the same directly to the _____ County Treasurer and provide proof of payment to the Vendor.

6. Insurance and Maintenance

The Vendee shall keep the premises insured for at least ____ thousand Dollars ($_____) against fire and extended coverage for the benefit of both parties, as their interest may appear, and provide a copy of the said policy to the Vendor or any mortgage.

The Vendee shall keep the building in a good state of repair at the Vendee's expense. At such time as the Vendor inspects the premises and finds that repairs are necessary, Vendor shall request that these repairs be made within sixty (60) days at the Vendee's expense.

The Vendee has inspected the premises constituting the subject matter of this Land Installment Contract, and no representations have been made to the Vendee by the Vendor in regard to the condition of said premises; it is agreed that the said premises are being sold to the Vendee as the same now exists and that the Vendor shall have no obligation to do or furnish anything toward the improvement of said premises. Vendor shall furnish a clear termite report at Vendor's expense prior to executing this contract. If the property has live infestation of wood-destroying organisms, Vendor will pay costs of treatment and repair damages caused by same. If Vendor elects not to do so, Vendee may elect to waive Vendor's responsibility and proceed, or Vendee may elect not to proceed with this contract.

7. Possession
The Vendee shall be given possession of the earlier described premises at Contract execution and shall thereafter have and hold the same subject to the provisions for default hereinafter set forth.

8. Delivery of Deed
Upon full payment of this contract, Vendor shall issue a General Warranty deed to the Vendee, free of all encumbrances except as otherwise set forth. In addition, Vendee reserves the right to convert this contract into a note and mortgage and receive a Warranty Deed to Vendee or assigns from Vendor, anytime the following conditions have been met by the Vendee:

1. At least 20 percent of the purchase price has been paid to Vendor.

2. Vendee is willing to pay all the costs of title transfer and document preparations.

The note and mortgage will bear the same terms as this contract for the remaining balance.

9. Default by Vendee
If an installment payment to be made by the Vendee under the terms of this Land Contract is not paid by the Vendee when due or within two (2) installments thereafter, the entire unpaid balance shall become due and collectable at the election of the Vendor, and the Vendor shall be entitled to all the remedies provided for by the laws of this state and/or to do any other remedies and/or relief now or hereafter provided for by law to such Vendor; and in the

event of the breach of this contract and any other respect by the Vendee, Vendor shall be entitled to all relief now or hereinafter provided for by the laws of this state.

Waiver by the Vendor of a default or a number of defaults in the performance hereof by the Vendee shall not be construed as a waiver of any default, no matter how similar.

10. General Provisions

There are no known pending orders issued by any governmental authority with respect to this property other than those spelled out in the Land Installment Contract prior to closing date for execution of the contract.

It is agreed that this Land Installment Contract shall be binding upon each of the parties, their administrators, executors, legal representatives, heirs, and assigns.

IN WITNESS WHEREOF, the parties have set their hands this _____ day of _____, 20_____.

Signed in the presence of: Vendor:

_____   _____

_____   _____

Signed in the presence of: Vendee:

_____   _____

_____   _____

STATE OF: _____

COUNTY OF: _____

On this _____ day of _____, 20_____, before me, a Notary Public in and for said county and state, personally came, _____ Vendor(s) and _____ Vendee(s) in the foregoing Land Installment Contract, and acknowledged the signing thereof to be their voluntary act and deed.

WITNESS my official signature and seal on the last day mentioned previously.

Notary Public _____

State of: _____

My commission expires: _____

WARRANTY DEED TO TRUSTEE

The Grantor(s) _____ of the County of _____
and the State of _____ for and in consideration
_____ Dollars, and other good and valuable considerations in
hand paid, conveys, grants, bargains, sells, aliens, remises, releases, confirms, and warrants under provisions of Section ____.

Unto _____ as Trustee and not personally under the
provisions of a trust agreement dated the ____ day of _____,
20____, known as Trust Number ____, the following described
real estate in the County of _____ State of
_____, to wit:

Together with all the tenements, hereditaments, and appurtenances thereto, belonging or in anywise appertaining.

To have and to hold the said premises in fee simple forever, with
the appurtenances attached thereto upon the trust and for the uses
and purposes herein and in said Trust Agreement set forth.

Full power and authority granted to said Trustee, with respect to
the said premises or any part of it, and at any time or times, to
subdivide said premises or any part thereof, to dedicate parks,
streets, highways, or alleys, and to vacate any subdivision or part
thereof, and to resubdivide said property as often as desired, to
contract to sell, to grant options to purchase, to sell on any terms
to convey either with or without consideration, to donate, to mortgage, to pledge, or to otherwise encumber said property, or any
part thereof, to lease said property, or any part, from time to time,
in possession or reversion by leases to commence now or later and
upon any terms and for any period or periods of time and to renew
or extend leases upon any terms and for any period or periods of
time to renew or extend leases upon any terms and for any period
or periods of time, and to amend, change, or modify and the terms
and provisions thereof at any time hereafter, to contract to make
leases and to grant options to lease and options to renew leases
and options to purchase the whole or any part of the reversion and
to contract respecting the manner of fixing the amount of future
renters to partition or to exchange the said property or any part

thereof for other real or personal property, to grant easements or changes of any kind, to release, convey, or assign any right, title, or interest in or about easement appurtenant to said premises or any part, and to deal with said property and every part thereof in all other ways and for such other considerations as it would be lawful for any person owning the same to deal with the same, whether similar to or different from the ways heretofore specified, at any time or times hereafter.

In no case shall any party dealing with the said trustee in relation to said premises, to whom said premises or any part thereof shall be conveyed, contracted to be sold, leased or mortgaged by said trustee, be obliged to see to the application of any purchase money, rent, or money borrowed or advanced on said premises, or be obliged to see that the terms of this trust have been complied with, or be obliged to inquire into the necessity or expediency of any act of said trustee, or be obliged or privileged to inquire into any terms of said trust agreement; and every deed, mortgage, lease, or other instrument executed by said trustee in relation to said real estate shall be conclusive evidence in favor of every person relying upon or claiming under such conveyance, lease, or other instrument (a) that at the same time of delivery thereof, the Trust created by this Indenture and by said Trust Agreement was in full force and effect; (b) that such conveyance or other instrument was executed in full accordance if the trust's constitutions and limitations contained herein and thereunder trust agreement or in some amendment thereof and binding upon all beneficiaries thereunder; and (c) that said Trustee was duly authorized and empowered to execute and deliver every such deed, trust deed, lease, mortgage, and other instrument.

The interest of each and every beneficiary hereunder and of all persons claiming under them or any of them shall be only in the earning, avails, and proceeds arising from the sale or other disposition of said real estate, and such interest is hereby declared to be personal property. No beneficiary hereunder shall have any title or interest, legal or equitable, in or to said real estate as such, but only an interest in the earnings, avails and proceeds thereof as aforesaid.

And the grantor hereby covenants with said grantee that the grantor is lawfully seized of said land in fee simple, that the grantor has good right and lawful authority to sell and convey said land and will defend the same against the lawful claims of any persons whomsoever, and that the said land is free of all encumbrances, except taxes accruing subsequent to December 31.

In witness whereof, the said grantor has hereunto set their hands and seals this ____ day of _____, 20____.

Signed, sealed, and delivered in our presence:

_____

_____   Seal

_____

_____   Seal

State of _____

County of _____

I hereby certify that on this day, before me, an officer duly authorized in the State aforesaid to take acknowledgments, personally appeared _____ to me known as the person(s) described in and who executed the foregoing Instrument and _____ acknowledged before me that he executed the same.

Witness my hand and official seal in the County and State aforesaid this ____ day of _____, 20____.

Notary Public: _____

State of _____

My Commission Expires: _____

PROMISSORY NOTE

$_____ Dated: _____

Principal Amount: _____ State of: _____

FOR VALUE RECEIVED, the undersigned hereby jointly and severally promise to pay to the order of _____, the sum of _____ Dollars ($_____), together with interest thereon at the rate of ____ percent per annum on the unpaid balance. Said sum shall be paid in the manner following:

All payments shall be first applied to interest and the balance to principal. This note may be prepaid, at any time, in whole or in part, without penalty. All prepayments shall be applied in reverse order of maturity.

This note shall at the option of any holder hereof be immediately due and payable upon the failure to make any payment due hereunder within ____ days of its due date.

In the event this note shall be in default, and placed with an attorney for collection, then the undersigned agree to pay all reasonable attorney fees and costs of collection. Payments not made within five (5) days of due date shall be subject to a late charge of ____ percent of said payment. All payments hereunder shall be made to such address as may from time to time be designated by any holder hereof.

The undersigned and all other parties to this note, whether as endorsers, guarantors, or sureties, agree to remain fully bound hereunder until this note shall be fully paid and waive demand, presentment, and protest and all notices thereto and further agree to remain bound, notwithstanding any extension, renewal, modification, waiver, or other indulgence by any holder or upon the discharge or release of any obligor hereunder or to this note or upon the exchange, substitution, or release of any collateral granted as security for this note. No modification or indulgence by any hereof shall be binding unless in writing; any indulgence on any one occasion shall not be an indulgence for any other or future occasion. Any modification or change of terms hereunder granted by any holder hereof, shall be valid and binding upon each of the undersigned, notwithstanding the acknowledgment of any of the undersigned, and each of the undersigned does hereby irrevocably grant to each of the others a power of attorney to enter into any such modification on their behalf. The rights of any holder hereof shall be cumulative and not necessarily successive. This note shall take effect as a sealed instrument and shall be construed, governed, and enforced in accordance with the laws of the State first appearing at the head of this note. The undersigned hereby execute this note as principals and not as sureties.

Signed in the presence of:

_____   _____

_____   _____

GUARANTEE

We the undersigned jointly and severally guarantee the prompt and punctual payment of all monies due under the aforesaid now and agree to remain bound until fully paid.

Signed in the presence of:

_____   _____

_____   _____

POWER OF ATTORNEY

KNOW ALL MEN BY THESE PRESENTS, that as principal (the "Principal") I, _____ of _____, have made, constitute, and appoint _____ as my true and lawful attorney ("Attorney"). Attorney is authorized in Attorney's absolute discretion from time to time and at any time with respect to any property, real or personal, at any time owned or held by me and without authorization of any court and in addition to any other rights, powers, or authority granted by any other provision of this power of attorney or by statute or general rules of law (and whether I am mentally incompetent, physically or mentally disabled, or incapable of managing my property and income), with full power of substitution, as follows:

1. To do and perform all and every act, deed, matter, and thing whatsoever in and about my estate, property, and affairs as fully and effectually to all intents and purposes as I might or could do in my own proper person, if personally present, the specifically enumerated powers described hereafter being in aid and exemplification of the full, complete, and general power herein granted and not in limitation or definition thereof.

2. To demand, sue for, and receive all debts, moneys, securities of money, goods, chattels, legacies, or other personal property to which I am now or may hereafter become entitled, or which are now or may become due, owing or payable to me from any person or persons whomsoever, and in my name to give effectual receipts and discharges for the same.

3. To borrow from time to time such sums of money and upon such terms as the said attorney may think expedient for or in relation to any of the purposes or objects aforesaid, or for any other purpose, upon the security of any of my property, whether real or personal, and for such purposes to give and execute open or unsecured notes and acknowledge mort-

gages or trust deeds with such powers and provisions as they may think proper, as well as such notes or bonds as it is necessary or proper to use therewith.

4. In my name, and as my act and deed, to sign, seal, acknowledge, and deliver all such leases and agreements as shall be requisite, or as my said attorney shall deem necessary or proper in the care and management of my estate; and to receive and collect all the rents that may be payable to me, and in my name to sign effectual receipts for the same.

5. To manage and superintend all of my real property whosesoever situates and found and to erect, pull down, and repair houses or other buildings, or machinery or otherwise improve any of the premises, and to insure the buildings against damage by fire and windstorm.

6. To subdivide, develop real property to public use or to make or obtain the vacation of plats and adjust boundaries, to adjust differences in valuation on exchange or partition by giving or receiving consideration, and to dedicate easements to public use without consideration.

7. To make, draw, sign, or endorse in my name any checks, drafts, bills of exchange, or promissory notes in which I shall be interested or concerned, or which shall be requisite in or about my business.

8. To sell and dispose of such shares of stock as I now hold or may hereafter hold in any business corporation, or any bonds or securities of the United States or any state, municipal corporation, or private company, and to receive the consideration money for the sale thereof, and for me and in my name to transfer such shares, bonds, or securities to the purchaser or purchasers thereof.

9. To vote in person or by proxy upon any item of security or property owned by me; to agree to the reorganization, merger, or consolidation of any corporation whose stock is owned by me, and to unite, in their discretion, with other

owners of similar property in carrying out any plan, making any change, giving any assent, and paying any sums of money affecting such securities or property, and, generally, to exercise in respect thereof the same rights and powers as are or may be lawfully exercised by persons owning similar property in their own right, and incident thereto, to accept in exchange for such stock or securities or other property, other stock, securities, or property, whether legal investments or not, in such reorganized or new corporation.

10. To invest and reinvest all or any part of my property in any property and undivided interests in property, wherever located, including bonds; debentures; notes, secured or unsecured; stocks of corporations regardless of class; interests in limited partnerships; real estate or any interest in any real estate, whether productive at the time of investment or not; interests in trusts; investment trusts, whether of the open and/or closed fund types; and participation in common, collective, or pooled trust funds or annuity contracts without being limited by any statute or rule of law concerning investments by fiduciaries.

11. To purchase for my benefit and in my behalf United States Government bonds, redeemable at par in payment of United States estate taxes imposed at my death upon my estate.

12. To obtain entry to and enter any lockbox in any bank or trust company wherein I may have leased or rented same, and to place therein my papers, instruments, bonds, securities, or other property belonging to me or to remove any such papers, instruments, bonds, securities, or other property therefrom.

13. To bargain, sell, grant, and convey to such person or persons, and for such sum or sums of money or other consideration or considerations as my said attorney shall deem most for my advantage and profit, any and all of my property, real, personal, or mixed, whosesoever situate and found; to make all necessary deeds and conveyances thereof, with such

covenants, warranties, and assurances as my said attorney shall deem expedient; to sign, seal, acknowledge, and deliver the same; to accept and receive the sum or sums of money or other consideration or considerations which shall be coming to me on account of such sale or sales.

14. To commence, prosecute, or enforce, or to defend, answer, or oppose, all actions or other legal proceedings touching any of the matters aforesaid, or any other matters in which I am or may hereafter be interested or concerned; and also, if it shall seem best, to compromise, refer to arbitration, or submit to judgment in any such action or proceeding.

15. To adjust, settle, compromise, or submit to arbitration any accounts, debts, claims and demands, disputes, and matters, touching any of the matters aforesaid, or any other matters that are now subsisting or may hereafter arise between me and any other person or persons or between my said attorney or any other person or persons.

16. To appoint and employ counsel, agents, servants, or other persons, at such salary or for such compensation as my said attorney may think proper, and to dismiss or discharge them and appoint or employ others in their place and stead.

17. To sign and execute in my name and as my act and deed all state and federal income tax returns, both preliminary and final, and to appear for me and represent me before the Treasury Department in connection with any matter involving federal taxes for any year whatsoever, in which I am a party, giving my said attorney full power to do everything whatsoever requisite and necessary to be done in the premises and to receive refund checks, to execute waivers of the Statute of Limitations, and to execute closing agreements, as fully as the undersigned might do if done in his own capacity, with full power of substitution and revocation, at any time subsequent to the date hereof and prior to the revocation hereof.

18. To make gifts of property, both real and personal, to my children (including Attorney), grandchildren and their spouses,

or any trusts created for their benefit, provided, however, that no single gift during any calendar year shall exceed the Federal Gift Tax Annual Exclusion then in effect for such year (or twice such amount if my spouse consents to having such gift treated as made one-half by her pursuant to Section 2513 of the Internal Revenue Code, as amended). For the purposes of this limitation, a gift in trust shall be deemed a gift to each of the beneficiaries.

19. To employ and compensate medical personnel including physicians, surgeons, dentists, medical specialists, nurses, and paramedical assistants deemed by Attorney needful for the proper care, custody, and control of my person and to do so without liability for any neglect, omission, misconduct, or the fault of any such physician or other medical personnel, provided such physician or other medical personnel were selected and retained with reasonable care, and to dismiss any such persons at any time, with or without cause.

20. To authorize any and all kinds of medical procedures and treatment including, but not limited to, medication, therapy, surgical procedures, and dental care, and to consent to all such treatment, medication, or procedures where such consent is required; to obtain the use of medical equipment, devices, or other equipment and devices deemed by Attorney needful for proper care, custody, and control of my person and to do so without liability for any neglect, omission, misconduct, or fault with respect to such medical treatment or other matters authorized herein.

In connection with the exercise of the powers herein described, Attorney is fully authorized and empowered to perform any other acts or things necessary, appropriate, or incidental thereto, with the same validity and effect as if I were personally present, competent, and personally exercised the powers myself. All acts lawfully done by Attorney hereunder during any period of my disability or mental incompetence shall have the same effect and inure to the benefit of and bind me and my heirs, devisees, legatees, and personal representatives as if I were mentally competent and not disabled. The powers herein conferred may be exercised by Attorney alone and the signature or act of Attorney on my behalf may be accepted by third persons as fully authorized by me and with the same force and effect as if done under my hand and seal and as if I were present in person, acting on my own behalf and competent. No person who may act in reliance upon the representations of Attorney for the scope of authority granted to Attorney shall incur any liability to me or to my estate as a result of permitting Attorney to exercise any power, nor shall any person dealing with Attorney be responsible to determine or insure the proper application of funds or property.

My mental or physical debility subsequent to my execution of the within power of attorney shall not revoke said power, which shall remain in full force and effect notwithstanding said mental or physical debility.

These presents shall extend to and be obligatory upon the executors, administrator, legal representatives, and successors, respectively, of the parties hereto.

IN TESTIMONY WHEREOF, I have hereunto affixed my signature this the _____ day of _____, 20____.

STATE OF: _____
COUNTY OF: _____

On this _____ day of _____, 20____, before me, a Notary Public in and for said State and County, duly commissioned and qualified, personally appeared, to me known to be the person described in and who executed the foregoing instrument, and acknowledged that he executed the same as his own free act and deed.

WITNESS my hand and Notarial Seal at office the day and year first previously written.

Notary Public: _____
State of: _____
My Commission Expires: _____

Appendix: Sample Forms and Procedures

PROPERTY ACQUISITION WORKSHEET

ADDRESS: _____

Estimated sales price after fix-up $_____

Down payment	
Closing costs	
Commission	
Appraisal	
Termite	
Miscellaneous	
Total expense to buy	

Rehab budget	
Cost overruns ($\pm$10%)	
Total rehab costs	

Payments for ____ months	
Property tax	
Insurance	
Total holding costs (+ your time and cost of your capital)	

Sale closing costs	
Commission	
Advertising, telemarketing	
Total sales costs	

$ Mortgage payoffs	
Total sales price	
Expense to buy	
Total rehab costs	
Total holding costs	
Total sales costs	

Your profit = $_____.

HIRING CONTRACTORS
Policy and Procedures

1. All proposed work to be performed for COMPANY will be submitted by written bid prior to any work being performed.

2. All part-time workers or bidders hired by COMPANY are independent subcontractors and are responsible for their own insurance and tax requirements. No worker or bidder shall hold COMPANY and Investment Corp. liable for any claims arising from any cause on any job. The liability for each job shall be the sole responsibility of the bidder alone.

3. NO check will be issued to any worker upon demand. Paid-on-completion jobs will be paid by check—AFTER inspection, after presentation of a proper invoice, within five (5) working days by mail.

4. NO checks will be mailed without an invoice.

5. NO checks will be written to walk-ins on demand.

6. Inspections are as follows—**NO EXCEPTIONS:**

   - *Roof.*   AFTER first significant rainfall or Metro Codes.*

   - *Electrical.*   AFTER final inspection and white tag from Metro Codes.

   - *Plumbing.*   AFTER full inspection of both supply and drainpipes and all fixtures or Metro Codes if applicable.

   - *HVAC.*   AFTER five days of continuous operation or verification of proper permit and subsequent final by Metro Codes.

   - *Hauling/trash disposal.*   AFTER dump receipts and invoice(s) are furnished.

7. All invoices should be mailed to COMPANY or left in the mailbox at COMPANY ADDRESS.

Metro Codes inspection means: Cleared and released on their computers and the appropriate utility.

8. All calls from workers concerning the job or payment for work completed should be made during normal business hours, Monday through Friday, unless other instructions are given.

9. NO draws or advancements of any kind will be made to any worker for any reason other than those agreed on in a bid or other arrangement in writing—**NO EXCEPTIONS.**

DO NOT WALK IN AND REQUEST A CHECK—
ALL CHECKS WILL BE MAILED.

10. No tools will be furnished by COMPANY to any worker. Should an exception be made for an emergency, the worker is to be completely responsible for the tool(s). Should they be lost or damaged, COMPANY will deduct the amount necessary to replace the tool(s) from the worker's paycheck.

11. ALL BIDS must include a start date, estimate of time to complete, and a finish date. ALL BIDDERS must adjust their schedules to finish ON TIME. Work not performed within the bidder's own agreed schedule will be penalized at a rate of 5 percent (5%) per day of the total bid until completion. THIS WILL BE ENFORCED!

12. Any bidder who pulls off in the middle of a job WILL BE LIABLE for any difference in his bid and what it costs COMPANY to finish the job, plus the 5% per day penalty until the job is restarted with a suitable replacement.

13. Any bidder who agrees to perform work for COMPANY will NOT be allowed to subcontract the work to someone else without the written permission of COMPANY. The bidder is to be on the job site to perform the work HIMSELF and oversee his helpers.

14. Should any bidder hire helpers, they shall be the sole responsibility of the bidder, and he alone assumes all liability for them.

15. All work performed by bidder shall be in a quality workmanlike manner. The use of substandard materials, fewer materi-

als than considered normal, or any attempt to cover up poor workmanship or inferior materials will result in immediate termination of the bidder—ON THE SPOT.

16. Any dispute over quality or workmanship will be resolved by the use of a for-hire independent inspectors' licensed contractor who is an expert in the category of the dispute, or a Metro Codes inspector.

17. The use, possession, presence, or the obvious effects of the use of any drugs or alcohol on any job site for COMPANY will be cause for IMMEDIATE TERMINATION—**NO EXCEPTIONS!**

18. Should any worker or bidder cause any damage to any part of the job site while performing their work, COMPANY will have the damage repaired and deduct that amount from the worker's paycheck.

THE FOLLOWING INFORMATION MUST BE COMPLETED BEFORE ANY BID IS CONSIDERED OR ACCEPTED OR ANY WORK IS PERFORMED:

1. Bidder's name:

2. Driver's license:

3. State:

4. Date of birth:

5. SS#:

6. Car license:

7. Make and model of car:

8. Phone number:

9. Current address:

10. One reference: Name: _____ Ph. #: _____

I have read this entire agreement and agree to all conditions. I understand and will abide by the preceding rules.

I understand and agree to all pay schedules, inspection procedures, and penalties for late or noncompletion.

I understand that I am, alone, responsible for all taxes, insurance, and liabilities for myself and anyone I hire.

I will not hold COMPANY or any property owner responsible for any damages or liabilities on this job.

I understand that I cannot perform any work that is not bid in writing—and accepted in writing.

I understand that I cannot perform any work until this agreement is filled out completely and signed.

This is the only agreement between myself and COMPANY—there are no others—either implied, oral, or written.

Worker or Bidder: _____

Date:_____

REHAB WORKSHEET

1. CASH OUT OF POCKET	
Down payment	
Closing costs	
Appraisal	
Termite letter	
Survey	
Title insurance	
Miscellaneous	
TOTAL	
2. COST OF REHAB	
Flooring	
Painting	
Roofing	
Windows/screens	
Kitchen (e.g., faucets, cabinets)	
Bathroom (e.g., vanity, sink, tub)	
Bedrooms	
Decorations (e.g., ceiling fans, brass)	
Doors	
Foundation	
Fireplace	
Plumbing	
Insulation	
Subtotal: Total multiplied by a 15% repair cost overrun	
TOTAL	

(Continued)

3. ESTIMATED HOLDING COSTS	
No. of months × mortgage	
+ Insurance	
+ Taxes	
+ Utilities	
TOTAL	
4. ESTIMATED SELLING COSTS (following rehab)	
Closing costs	
Attorneys' fees	
Document/transfer	
Taxes	
Commissions	
TOTAL	
5. TOTAL ESTIMATED. ACQUISITION, REHAB, HOLDING, and SELLING COSTS (Add totals from 1,2,3, and 4)	
5a. Plus (+) mortgage balance payoff	
6. TOTAL COST OF PROPERTY (Add lines 5 and 5a)	
7. TOTAL PROJECTED SELLING PRICE (following rehab)	
8. TOTAL PROFIT (Subtract line 6 from line 7)	

PROCEDURES FOR CONTRACTORS

There are no exceptions to the following policies and procedures:

- All contracts must be in writing and as detailed as possible.
- No checks will be issued without written contracts and invoices.
- Regarding draws, a maximum of one-third (⅓) of the total bid will be given up front to cover materials. The balance will not be paid until all work is complete. Absolutely complete. If one doorknob is loose, or one sink has a small leak, the balance will not be paid.
- The balance will not be paid until all of the contractor's trash is removed.
- Service calls will not be paid until they are completed and verified by the tenant that they are complete.
- Contractor will give a date for the completion of a job. If the job is not complete, then the landlord loses money by not being able to rent out the property. Therefore, a $50.00 per day penalty will be deducted from the contractor's final draw for each day, including weekends, that the job is not done.
- On houses for Section 8, 20 percent of the total will be held back until the unit passes the Section 8 inspection.
- A $25 bonus will be paid for units that pass the Section 8 inspection the first time.
- Contractor will guarantee work for six months.
- Contractor must show proof of workers' compensation insurance. If not, the premiums will be deducted from the cost of the job and paid by the owner or property manager.
- All contractors must sign and agree to this contractor's agreement and attached agreement regarding liability and contractor's status as a contractor and not an employee.

OWNER MANAGER   CONTRACTOR

_____   _____

LOAN QUALIFICATION WORKSHEET

The following worksheet will allow you to calculate the mortgage loan amount for which you qualify.

Maximum debt allowed

Stable monthly income	$_____
(Multiply by 0.28)	×28%
Maximum monthly housing expense	$_____
Stable monthly income	$_____
(Multiply by 0.36)	×36%

Maximum monthly housing expense

Plus other obligations	$_____

Monthly housing expense		Total monthly expenses	
Principal + interest	$_____	Total housing	$_____
Real estate taxes	$_____	Installment debt	$_____
Insurance premium	$_____	Revolving charges	$_____
Homeowner's		Alimony, etc.	$_____
association	$_____		
Other	$_____		
Total	$_____	Total	$_____

Compare actual to maximum expenses allowed. Actual expenses should not exceed the maximum allowed. These qualifications are the standard current guidelines used by most lenders in your area.

INFORMATION SHEET FOR NOTES (LOANS)

Holder: _____

Date: _____

Name: _____

Address: _____

Phone: _____ Source: _____

Note (Original) (Now) (First)
    Balance: (PV)
    Interest rate: (I)
    Payment amount: (PMT)
    Term: (N)
    Balloons: (FV)
    Present loan constant %:
    Creation date:
    Number of payments remaining:
    Why holder is selling:
    Seller needs: $____ (YTM) ____% How soon? ____

Property
    Address: _____
    Property type: _____ Age: _____

Condition: _____
    Sale price $: _____
    Down payment $: _____

LTV ratio %: _____ Payor occupied? _____

Documents from seller (copies)
    Title policy and report
    Appraisal report
    Deed of trust (mortgage)
    Senior liens

Settlement sheet
    Deed

Fire/liability policy: _____

Appointment
    Date:
    Time:

Location: _____

Offered (or next step in the process): _____

Agreed contract purchase price: $_____

Settlement date: _____

Closer: _____ Phone number: _____

Settlement location: _____

Additional information: _____

LEASE-OPTION PROSPECT QUALIFICATION FORM

Name   Date/Time

Phone   Regarding Rating

Second Applicant's Name   Other Applicants   Pets

Are you looking to rent or own?

Have you seen the house? Y or N

Where do you live now?   How long there?

Is it a house or apartment? ____

How much do you pay now?

Have you ever been late with your payment?

Have you ever been evicted?

Is your landlord aware that you will be moving?

Employer/Position

How long there?   Gross salary?

Spouse Employer/Position

How long there?   Gross salary?

How is your credit?   How is your spouse's credit?

When can you move in?

What is the most you can pay per month?

How much money do you have to put down on your new home?

Can you pay extra per month to build up a down payment?

We know the bank requires this, and you won't ever be able to buy if we don't work out a down payment plan.

Tax return

We want you to succeed in having your own home!

LETTER TO POTENTIAL INVESTORS TO SELL A PROPERTY

Note: You can try a number of versions of this sample offer geared to any number of different types of investors (e.g., real estate club members, nonprofits).

Dear _____,

I'm writing to urge you to take immediate action on a wonderful opportunity that just became available. Here's what it's all about: I have a piece of property that I've purchased recently, that almost any astute, no-nonsense investor would find an exceptional value. I have completely rehabilitated the house and would welcome your inspecting any structural portion or mechanical system of the property. There are no serious defects, and the asking price is well below normal market value.

It is my opinion that, over any number of years of ownership, this property is going to give someone peace of mind knowing it is a sound financial investment. I will give you a call in the next few days to see if you have an interest. If you want even more prompt action, my telephone number is _____. Or, if you would like, I have prepared a fact sheet on this property and will send it to you upon request.

If I can be of help to you in answering any questions you might have regarding this property, please call me. I will also include a bit of information about the work that we do in the area, the people we help, and the solutions we provide for individuals and non-profit organizations.

By the way, I realize that you may not know me, but I am familiar with your community. As a member of the community, I should tell you this: The kind of relationships I am seeking, whether you have an interest in this property or not, is a long and enduring one. I really only want to sell you something that meets your precise needs.

The fact is, from time to time, I'd be happy simply to show you some of the unique properties I uncover in the marketplace that go unrecognized. Of course, I won't be offended if you buy from someone else. Actually, I may advise you against certain properties, even though it might be in my interest to do otherwise.

It is the long-term relationship that meets the test of time that I want to maintain. I can also assure you I will make available my best deals even if we never make contact again. I will make sure that the only situations I show you are those that are in your self-interest. I don't want you to ever make any errors and, frankly, I don't want to make any myself.

Sincerely,

Your Name

Follow-Up to Letter

Here's a suggested telescript for following up: "Mr. Jones, this is Sally Robbins. I am calling you to see if you received the letter I sent regarding a piece of property that is now available and whether you had any questions about it. I am on a tight schedule but would be delighted to take the time to answer any questions that you might have regarding the property."

LETTER TO INSURER TO PUT OWNER'S NAME ON POLICY

Note: If you have an interest in a property, make sure you are named as an insured party. Here is an example of a letter you might write to the company that insures your property, or make sure the seller writes and sends it on your behalf.

(date)

XYZ Insurance Company
123 Jump Street
Anytown, VA

    RE: Policy Number _____
    Policy Name _____
    Property Owner _____
    Property Address _____

Dear Sirs:

You are hereby notified that an interest in a deed of trust secured by the above property has been purchased by _____.

Please add the below-named as beneficiary to the above described policy as loss payee.

Should there be a lapse of insurance due to a nonpayment of the premium, please notify the note purchaser at the address below.

Sincerely,

Signed: seller of the note

Information about the purchaser (new beneficiary):

Name:
Mailing address:
Telephone:

Appendix: Guidelines for Success

GUIDELINES FOR
SUCCESSFUL NEGOTIATING

- Ask kind and understanding questions: Use them to gather information. Probe until you fully understand the seller's situation.

- Listen carefully to the answers, but remember to listen to and trust your inner (gut) feeling too.

- Use sensitive questioning and listening to identify what the seller really needs and what his/her motivation is. Learn to describe the benefits of your offer in terms of the seller's needs.

- Use your experience and your creativity! There are as many potential solutions as there are needs. Offer no more than is necessary to fulfill the needs.

Improve your negotiating skills further by remembering these valuable rules:

- The one who mentions price or terms first loses.

- Always find out what else the seller can add to the transaction.

- Determine if the seller doesn't need all the cash now—use that knowledge to your advantage!

- Use questions. Avoid declarative sentences.

- When someone answers no, ask, "Why not?"

- Frame your questions to get the answers you want. People are much more motivated to respond with a no than a yes. Make that no mean yes by posing your question like this: "Is there any reason why we couldn't consider . . . ?" If no is the answer you get, move on to your proposal.

- Be aware of body language—your own and the seller's. It reveals subconscious thoughts and feelings.

- Never be afraid of silence. Once you have asked a question, *wait* for the answer, no matter how long it takes. Remember, if you are talking, you are not learning. If you must say something, choose your words very carefully.

- Make promises slowly and thoughtfully—they are the foundation of your reputation.

- Never burn your bridges. He or she who becomes angry is out of control and always loses.

- If the deal suits your needs, get a contract (subject to verification of the information) or an option for a period of time long enough to verify every detail.

- If the deal does not suit your needs, always pursue an option. This will give you time to rethink your position and to see if someone else might like to pursue the opportunity.

Negotiating Keys

Key 1. Stick to questions.

Key 2. Listen to the answers.

Key 3. Try to fully understand the situation.

Key 4. Be friendly, but really listen.

Key 5. Try to determine what the problem really is.

Key 6. Why are they selling their paper?

Key 7. Do not think about potential solutions until you are certain you and they understand their problem.

Key 8. How much and how soon do they need the money?

Key 9. Remember: Talk about your benefits in terms of their needs.

Key 10. Keep your financial calculator out of sight.

PROPERTY BUSINESS PLAN EXAMPLE

Greenwood Court Project

Brief Description

Sixteen brick duplexes, each containing two 2-bedroom, 1-bath apartments of about 850 square feet, located in a nice area of East Nashville. All but about eight units are rented for between $355.00 and $400.00 per month. Over 90 percent of the tenants are on the Section 8 program, which means the government pays all or most of the rent. All of the tenants and rents qualify as low or very low income according to the Department of Housing and Urban Development.

The vacancies are due to the fact that they are the last ones to be rehabilitated. All of the other units have just gone through a major rehabilitation. The units are located in a court that dead-ends, enabling the owner to control the area.

Long-Term Plan

To rent the majority of the units to Section 8 tenants. Some of the units may be converted to three bedrooms to increase the rents to about $450.00 per side rather than $375.00 per side. The cost to do this is about $1,000 per unit. Though demand for two-bedroom units is high, the demand for three-bedroom units is incredibly high.

The Section 8 Program

This program is for low-income families, mainly led by single mothers with children. The money is allotted for 10 years for each certificate holder or tenant by HUD and is administered by MDHA.

The leases are guaranteed for one year. Usually, the government pays all of the rent. Sometimes the tenant has to pay a small amount. MDHA inspects the units twice a year and requires them to be in good repair.

Section 8 and MDHA also insure against damages for up to two months' rent, about $750.00 for each unit. If the tenant damages the unit, the landlord can collect the damage money from Section 8.

The demand for available Section 8 housing is very high. Thus, I have been operating my 20 duplexes at a 100 percent occupancy rate with waiting lists for each property. The landlord can screen the tenants and does not have to rent to someone to whom he or she does not want to rent.

Financial Detail

Per-building purchase price	$39,000.00
18% down payment	7,020.00
Amount financed	31,980.00
Monthly payment, 15 years at 8.5% interest	314.92
Taxes per month	40.00
Insurance per month	25.00
Monthly payment with taxes and insurance	379.92
Current rent per duplex	750.00
Free cash flow per month	370.08

Risks

Vacancy and repair risks are inherent in real estate. The vacancy risk should be about zero. Again, the demand for Section 8 housing is high. I have not advertised in almost a year and have kept my 20 duplexes full. I get about 10 to 20 calls a week from people looking for housing. Furthermore, the Greenwood Project is in an excellent location. The repair cost is also minimal because Section 8 guarantees about two months' rent for damage repair. That is about $750.00 per unit. All of my appliances are insured, so it is very difficult for a tenant to do more than $750.00 worth of damage, especially if they are managed properly. Also, only one side of each duplex has to stay rented in order to pay the note, taxes, and insurance.

Management

I personally manage all of my properties. I walk through each unit at least once every 30 days. I have and intend to provide the highest-quality low- and moderate-income housing in Davidson County. All of my units are like new when the tenants move in, and I try to keep them that way.

I use licensed, bonded contractors for all of my repairs. They work for about $7.00 per hour and do quality work. Thus, whatever repairs I do incur are handled promptly, professionally, and reasonably.

FORMULATING
A WINNING STRATEGY

6 months   1 year   5 years   10 years   20 years

Personal goals, your health: _____

_____

Mental education: _____

_____

Spiritually: _____

_____

Family, you and your family: _____

_____

Vacation, travel plans: _____

_____

Fun, hobbies: _____

_____

Monetary, career: _____

_____

Charitable goals, helping others: _____

_____

Current job
Monthly income: _____   Annual income: _____
Current savings: _____   Current expenses: _____
Job satisfaction: 1–10: _____

Current credit: Excellent   Good   Fair   Bad

Investment savings
Car: _____
IRA: _____
Employee programs: _____
Cash: _____
Stocks/bonds: _____ Average yield: _____
Real estate: _____
Other: _____

Personality type
Analytical
Love to deal with people

Love to work with numbers, programs
Love to work with hands
Love to be alone
Great with big picture
Great with details

Available amount of money to invest in real estate
(Remember to keep a cushion)

Cash: _____   Brokerage loans: _____
Credit lines: _____   Private loans: _____
Equity line: _____   Family loans: _____
Unencumbered assets: _____   Credit cards (risky): _____
IRA: _____
Collateral to pledge for bank loans, real estate, stocks, bonds, and
financial statements: _____
Banking relationship: _____
Income goals: _____
Cash flow for real estate wealth accumulation: _____

WORKSHEET

	Annual Income Needs	Annual Income Goals	Actual Annual Income
Current	_____	_____	_____
1 year	_____	_____	_____
2 years	_____	_____	_____
3 years	_____	_____	_____
4 years	_____	_____	_____
5 years	_____	_____	_____
10 years	_____	_____	_____
15 years	_____	_____	_____
20 years	_____	_____	_____

Free hours, or hours available to spend on real estate weekly:
1–5   6–10   11–20   21–30   31–40   41–50   51–60   61–70   71–80

MY PLAN

Little or no capital/credit is required.

1. Flipping
   - Look at 20 houses.
   - Lock up three.
   - Flip one.
   - Average flip: $3,000 to $7,000.

2. Lease optioning
   - Call on 20 houses.
   - Negotiate with four.
   - Lease-option one.
   - Average monthly cash flow: $200 to $400.
   - Option profit: $500 to $3,000.
   - Beware of repair and vacancy.

3. Sandwich leasing
   - Call on 20 homes.
   - Negotiate with four.
   - Sandwich-lease with two.
   - Monthly cash flow $100 to $400.

4. Mortgage brokering
   - Search, advertise for mortgages.
   - Find two decent ones.
   - Close on one.
   - Average brokerage commission: $1,500 to $5,000.
   - May need license.

5. Brokering tax certificates

   - Research local rules. Find investor, bid at auction for investors. Can be complicated. Liability can be high. May need license, though I could make substantial commissions and find great deals to flip.

6. Private money brokering (may need a license)

   - Find lenders, find good loans.

   - 1 to 5 percent spread per month.

   - 1 to 10 points up front.

   - Example: Broker a $40,000 loan (at 11 to 13 percent for a 15-year loan), 5 points = $2,000 up front, 2 percent spread at $60 per month for the life of the loan.

7. Flipping with taking back a note or cash and a note

   - Flip property, take back a second mortgage as my commission. Cash and monthly income.

8. Real estate agent (license needed)—commissions

   - Average commissions on a sale are 5 to 7 percent. I may have to split commission, plus pay my brokerage 20 to 70 percent of my commission. Sell a $100,000 house with a 6 percent commission and I earn $6,000. I may have to split with other agents and my broker.

9. Consulting

   - Consult with investors, retirees, nonprofits, governmental agencies, real estate firms, estates, attorneys, CPAs, and financial planners; give seminars. Promotion costs may be high. My fees: $35 to $200 per hour or commissions; flip potentials.

10. Property management

    - Need legal entity. Bank accounts, computer (preferably). Liability insurance $800 to $2,000 annually. Receive 8 to 11 percent of rents collected monthly. May keep late fees, charge tenants $50 to $150 application fee. Charge $50 to

$150 lease renewal fee. Charge for and own my own maintenance company. May need to be a Realtor. Profits come with volume.

11. Maintenance company

- Make ready empty units. Apartment get-ready. Fix up and clean apartments and houses. I can do it, or hire a subcontractor at $8 to $10 per hour or by the job. Painting, carpet cleaning, rehabilitation, landscaping.

12. Contract for deed/lease options

- May be able to negotiate for little or no money down. I can control property, lease-option, or contract for deed for more money per month. Get option/deposit money up front.

    Example: I can lease-option or contract for deed a house for $40,000, with $500 down, $400 per month for 20 years. I turn around and lease-option/contract and deed it for $1,500 down, $600 a month. I make a $1,000 profit up front, an additional $200 a month profit for the next 20 years. Average up-front profit: $500 to $5,000. Average monthly profit: $100 to $500. Little or no landlord headaches if done correctly.

Cash, capital, and/or credit may be required.

1. Buy, rehabilitate, and sell.

- Need purchase money. May get owner's terms. Need money for repair costs and holding costs. Average rehab should net me at least $12,000, or about 30 percent of retail sales price. Alternative to cash: use investor's money, partner the deal, use equity sharing, or use credit lines.

2. Buy and hold real estate.

- May need cash for down payment and repairs. Great wealth accumulator. Great cash flow each month. Rule of thumb: a single-family house should have a cash flow of at least \$100 to \$150 per month before vacancy and repairs with a 65 to 75 percent loan on it.

- Duplexes should cash-flow about \$200 to \$400 per month before vacancy and repairs. Multifamily units depend on capitalization rates, type, and size. Management can be a headache. I can hire a manager for between 7 and 11 percent of gross monthly rents. Great for cash flow and wealth accumulation.

3. Buy and create paper by creative selling.

- I need cash or credit to buy and fix up. I then sell, taking some cash, a note, an installment deed, and/or a land contract. Generates profits and cash flow. Beware of the tax burdens that come with the profits. My notes that I hold are marketable. I can sell them at discounts to raise cash. Good monthly income. Few, if any, management headaches.